# INSIGHT GUIDES

# ITALIAN LAKES

## StepbyStep

Discovery
CHANNEL

APA PUBLICATIONS L
Part of the Langenscheidt Publishing Group

# CONTENTS

# ABOUT THIS BOOK

This *Step by Step Guide* has been produced by the editors of Insight Guides, whose books have set the standard for visual travel guides since 1970. With top-quality photography and authoritative recommendations, this guidebook brings you the very best of the Italian Lakes in a series of 18 tailor-made tours.

## WALKS AND TOURS

The tours in the book provide something to suit all budgets, tastes and trip lengths. As well as covering the Italian Lakes' many classic sights, the routes track lesser-known areas; there are also trips to Bergamo and Milan for those who wish to add a taste of urban chic to their trip.

The tours embrace a range of interests, so whether you are an art fan, a gourmet, a vinophile, a fashionista, a lover of gardens, or have kids to entertain, you will find an option to suit.

We recommend that you read the whole of a tour before setting out. This should help you to familiarise yourself with the route and enable you to plan where to stop for refreshments – options

**Above:** Gargnano on Lake Garda; Isola di San Giulio on Lake Orta; Villa del Balbianello; all aboard at Limone sul Garda; Tremezzo, Lake Como.

for this are shown in the 'Food and Drink' boxes, recognisable by the knife-and-fork sign.

For our pick of the walks by theme, consult Recommended Tours For… *(see pp.6–7).*

## OVERVIEW

The tours are set in context by this introductory section, giving an overview of the region to set the scene, plus background information on food and drink, shopping, entertainment, and sports and outdoor activities. A succinct history timeline in this chapter highlights the key events that have shaped the Italian Lakes region over the centuries.

## DIRECTORY

Also supporting the tours is a Directory chapter, comprising a clearly organised A–Z of practical information, our pick of where to stay while you are in the region and select restaurant listings; these eateries complement the more low-key cafés and restaurants that feature within the tours themselves, offering a wider choice for evening dining.

## The Author

Susie Boulton has travelled extensively in Italy for over 25 years, and has written and contributed to many of Insight's Italian titles. Susie first became acquainted with the Italian Lakes while working for *Holiday Which?* magazine, providing information on the cleanliness of lake waters, comfort of hotels and quality of regional cuisine. More recently, she wrote the Berlitz Pocket Guides to both Milan and the Italian Lakes. Whether for work or pleasure, Susie finds any excuse to revisit this sublime region of northern Italy.

Many of the tours in this book were originally conceived by Italy specialist Lisa Gerard-Sharp.

## Margin Tips
Shopping tips, historical facts, handy hints and information on activities help visitors make the most of their time in the Italian Lakes.

## Feature Boxes
Notable topics are highlighted in these special boxes.

## Key Facts Box
This box gives details of the distance covered on the tour, plus an estimate of how long it should take. It also states where the tour starts and finishes, and gives key travel information such as which days are best to do the tour or handy transport tips.

## Footers
Look here for the tour name, a map reference and the main attraction on the double page.

## Food and Drink
Recommendations of where to stop for refreshment are given in these boxes. The numbers prior to each restaurant/café name link to references in the main text. Restaurants are also plotted on lake and city maps.

Unless otherwise stated, restaurants are open daily for lunch and dinner. The € signs at the end of each entry reflect the approximate cost of a two-course à la carte dinner for one with half a bottle of house wine. These should be seen as a guide only. Price ranges, also quoted on the inside back flap for easy reference, are as follows:

**€€€€**  over 65 euros
**€€€**  45–65 euros
**€€**  25–45 euros
**€**  below 25 euros

## Route Map
Detailed cartography shows the tour clearly plotted with numbered dots. For more detailed mapping, see the pull-out map slotted inside the back cover.

## CASTLE ENTHUSIASTS

Lake Garda's shores (tour 15) are studded with medieval castles, built by the Scaligeri family from Verona; the best-preserved is the Rocca Scaligera at Sirmione (tour 14). Trentino (tour 17) is dotted with fortifications, while Angera (tour 2) is home to the imposing Rocca Borromeo.

# RECOMMENDED TOURS FOR...

### SHOPPING

Head to the factory outlets of Como (tour 9), 'City of Silk', for discounted designer clothes and accessories; or browse in the boutiques of Bellagio (tour 8) or Bergamo (tour 11).

### ESCAPING THE CROWDS

Take a dip in unspoilt Lake Mergozzo (tour 4), or spend time on the tranquil shores of Lake Iseo (tour 12). Relatively unexplored Franciacorta (tour 13) is a pretty region for touring.

### FERRY TRIPS

Sit back and let the ferries do the work for you. The cruises from Stresa to Locarno (tour 5), Como to Bellagio (tour 10) and Sirmione to Malcesine (tour 15) are among the most scenic.

### TOP VIEWS

For truly spectacular views of the lakes, take one of the cable-cars *(funivie)* that whisk you up to a mountain ridge or summit. Stresa's cable-car climbs up Monte Mottarone (tour 3), Malcesine's up Monte Baldo (tour 15) and Como's to the hill village of Brunate (tour 9).

## FOOD AND WINE

Vinophiles and gourmets alike will enjoy Franciacorta (tour 13), home of Italy's finest sparkling wine and many fine regional restaurants. Bergamo (tour 11) is a favourite for foodies, and the culinary scene in Milan (tour 18) caters for all tastes.

## ISLAND HOPPING

Follow the flow to the Borromean Islands (tour 1), the jewels of Lake Maggiore; visit Lake Orta's lovely Isola di San Giulio (tour 6), or take lunch on the Locanda dell'Isola restaurant on Como's Isola Comacina (tour 10). Hike or bike around Lake Iseo's Monte Isola (tour 12), and try out the local fish.

## ART LOVERS

View rich collections of Renaissance art, from Bergamo's Accademia Carrara (tour 11) to Milan's Museo Poldi Pezzoli and Pinacoteca di Brera, home to Leonardo da Vinci's *The Last Supper* (tour 18).

## SPIRITUALITY

At lovely Lake Orta (tour 6) visit the Sacro Monte devotional route and the peaceful island of San Giulio. On Lake Maggiore take a boat to Santa Caterina del Sasso (tour 3).

## VILLAS AND GARDENS

Immerse yourself in the lush gardens of famous villas: Lake Maggiore's showpiece is Villa Taranto (tour 4), while Lake Como boasts villas Carlotta, Melzi and Serbelloni (tour 8) and the movie regular Villa del Balbianello (tour 10).

# OVERVIEW

An overview of the region's geography, customs and culture, plus illuminating background information on food and drink, shopping, entertainment, sports and outdoor activities, and history.

# INTRODUCTION

*Blessed by a mild climate, romantic waterfront views and lush vegetation, the Italian Lakes have long been a favoured haunt of visitors from the north. Add sports, culture, fashion and gastronomy, and it is little wonder that the lakes today attract an ever increasing number of tourists.*

### Portrait of a Lake

Henry James's heart soared as he left Switzerland for the Italian Lakes: 'On, on into Italy we went – a rapturous progress through a wild luxuriance of corn and olives and figs and mulberries and chestnuts and frescoed villages and clamorous beggars and all the good old Italianisms of tradition.' The sight of sluggish steamers and snow-clad peaks still stirs visitors. But as James said of Lake Como, 'It's the place to enjoy *à deux* – it's a shame to be here in gross melancholy solitude.'

The deep glacial lakes of northern Italy lie between the southern foothills of the Alps, near the Swiss border, and the low-lying plains of the Po Valley. The famous trio are Lake Como, which lies north of the great metropolis of Milan, Lake Maggiore to the city's northwest and Lake Garda to the east. Although the lakes extend over four regions – Piedmont, Lombardy, Trentino and Veneto – the area is comparatively small and easily covered by car or public transport. The A4 autostrada provides a quick way of getting across the region, and for those who want to explore the shopping delights of Milan, the city is no more than an hour away from Stresa or Como by car or train.

### SHAPING THE LAKES

It was glaciers at the end of the last Ice Age that gouged out the ribbons of water that are now the lakes. For over 10,000 years inhabitants have also left their mark on the region, from the prehistoric rock engravings in the Camonica Valley to the remains of Roman villas to the castles and *palazzi* of the ruling dynasties. The Lombard plain was hardly ideal terrain on which to settle: the marshes needed to be drained and the water channelled into canals. Yet by medieval times it was domesticated and dotted with castles, churches, abbeys and palaces. The transformation, from bog to economic

**Right:** boarding at Como waterfront.

powerhouse, was thanks largely to the industriousness of the lakeside towns' natives and the advent of a prosperous local mercantile class.

## LOCAL CULTURE

The lakes region's complex culture can be divided into discrete mini-cultures. The four different regions of the lakes area all have clearly separate identities. But it is the bond with, and loyalty to, their home town that many Italians feel most deeply. The Comaschi (natives of Como), for example, live in close proximity to Milan, one of Europe's great cities, and yet, far from embracing the cosmopolitan life of the city, they identify only with their own town. Members of Como's old commercial families have known each other since infancy, and do business together in a relaxed way. Their commitment to local culture embraces everything from the local silk industry to an appreciation of the medieval craftsmen who built Como's Romanesque churches. The strong sense of regional identity is also reflected in the host of different dialects and cuisines within the region.

## VISITORS TO THE LAKES

The lakes have long cast a spell over visitors. The Romans were enamoured of the lakeside spas – Catullus owned a villa at Sirmione and Pliny the Younger built two villas at Bellagio. Travellers on the Grand Tour, after a treacherous journey over the Alps, were awestruck by the sudden vision of the sublime lakes and the Mediterranean flora that flourished on the shores. Shelley, Wordsworth and other Romantic poets were bewitched by the dramatic natural beauty of the deep-blue waters and mountain peaks; and Henry James was almost lost for words.

*Rich, Royal and Famous*
By the late 19th century the lakes had become a pleasure ground for the rich, royal and famous. In 1879 Queen Victoria stayed at Villa Clara at Baveno on Lake Maggiore. In the same decade Lake Garda – notably the resort of Arco in Trentino – became a retreat for Austrian grand-dukes. While the aristocracy of Mitteleuropa flocked to the sanatoria around Lake Garda, the lake was also appreciated by writers and politicians: the Grand Hotel in Gardone Riviera was patronised by Vladimir Nabokov and Somerset Maugham, and it became Winston Churchill's base for painting holidays.

**Above from far left:**
Tremezzo, Lake Como; mud treatment at a spa in Sirmione; castle at Arco; Bellagio, 'Pearl of Lake Como'.

**Below:** people and pooches.

## Villas and Gardens

The Baroque period was a golden era for construction; ostentatious villas and gardens embodied the aspirations of ambitious owners. With its landscaped hillside gardens, Villa Carlotta on Lake Como exudes panache *(see p.55)*, while Lake Maggiore's Isola Bella, its grounds full of statuary, fountains and grottoes, is a triumph of lofty terraces *(see p.29)*. For the wealthy, there are palatial villas converted to luxury hotels, such as the Villa d'Este at Cernobbio *(see p.114)* and the Grand Hotel Villa Serbelloni at Bellagio *(see p.115)*. Wherever you go, the gardens are always sumptuous, with exotic flora that thrives in the benign spring-to-autumn climate.

**Above from left:** waterfront café at Torbole; vineyard in Franciacorta; Laglio, George Clooney's summering spot; sunbathing and sailing on Lake Garda.

**Below:** figuring out ferry times.

LUINO

*Celebrity Status*

Today the lakes provide a weekend or holiday retreat for Milanese industrialists, film stars and fashion designers. Lake Como in particular is a favourite haunt of celebrities. George Clooney's purchase of a magnificent villa at Laglio in 2002 has sent prices rocketing (especially anywhere near Laglio), and other celebrities are following suit and snapping up some of the loveliest villas on the lake. The Villa del Balbianello has acquired celebrity status by featuring in a number of recent films *(see feature, p.63)*.

The lakes also feature in the recent James Bond movie, *Quantum of Solace* (2008), which opens with a dramatic car chase in the tunnels along the eastern shore of Lake Garda, culminating in a spectacular crash.

## A Long Life in Limone

The citizens of Limone sul Garda on the northwest shore of Lake Garda have one of the highest rates of life expectancy in Europe, with a large number of healthy residents over 80. The absence of heart disease here has been studied by many scientists, who variously ascribe this exceptional healthiness to climate, diet or genes. The village was isolated until the 1930s – only accessible by boat or by crossing the mountains – so the secret may lie in a limited gene pool and rare blood group. A mystery protein in the locals' blood, known as Apolipoprotein A-1 (or Apo A-1 Milano), appears to purge fat from the arteries and give a much reduced susceptibility to heart attacks and strokes. All the carriers are descendants from a couple who married in 1644. Genes aside, a mild climate, stress-free lifestyle and cholesterol-free diet of lemons, lake fish and olives all contribute to the fine health of Lake Garda's residents.

## WHICH LAKE?

There are six main holiday lakes, all quite different in character: Orta, Maggiore, Lugano, Como, Iseo and Garda (from west to east). German-orientated Lake Garda is the largest of the lakes and receives the most tourist visitors; its beaches, theme parks, sports and nightlife attract a younger crowd as well as families.

Lake Maggiore – famous for its jewel-like Borromean Islands and mountain-girt northern shores – is the second-largest lake, with its northern section lying in the Swiss canton of Ticino.

Lovely little Lake Orta lies to the west, and is noted for its spiritual air and excellent small hotels, while romantic Lake Como, north of Milan, offers dramatic scenery, quaint ports and *belle époque* villas. Captivating and tranquil Lake Iseo, between lakes Como and Garda, is the region's best-kept secret.

## GETTING AROUND

If you are planning to tour a number of lakes, renting a car is certainly the most convenient form of transport. However, driving along the lakeshores is not as leisurely as it may sound. Long stretches of the lakesides, including Como's eastern shore and much of Lake Maggiore's western one, are spoilt by heavy traffic along narrow and tortuous roads. Beware, too, of the dimly lit tunnels along the lakeshores.

## Better by Boat

A much more relaxing way of seeing the lakes is by boat. The first steamers on the lakes were launched in 1826, and boats have been ferrying passengers around ever since. The boats are still called steamers and they still chug from village to village, but nowadays they are large diesel-engined ships with a capacity of 500–1,000. In the early days most towns were without a landing stage, and rowing boats used to shuttle passengers and goods to and from the ferries. Today you can cruise around all the main lakes, stopping at almost every village. This is the best way to admire the fine mountain scenery and Riviera-like shores. Hydrofoils, which bypass the smaller ports, are the faster means of travel, enabling you to cover the entire length of the larger lakes in 2–3 hours.

## Getting High

Mountain cable-cars, whisking you from lakeside towns to mountain summits or ridges, provide another entertaining form of transport, with truly spectacular views. You can take these from Como, Stresa on Lake Maggiore and from Malcesine on Lake Garda.

## MILAN AND OTHER HISTORIC CITIES

Few visitors to the region can resist a day's shopping trip to Milan. The city is synonymous with fashion and packs all the top designer stores in one very exclusive quarter near the centre of the city called the Quadrilatero d'Oro (Golden Quadrangle). But Milan has artistic and architectural treasures as well, among them Leonardo da Vinci's *The Last Supper*, the masterpieces in the Brera Art Gallery and one of the largest and most sumptuous Gothic churches in Europe.

The southern stretches of the region are also home to artistically rich cities, such as Bergamo, Brescia, Mantua and Verona. With the exception of Verona, these historic cities are comparatively free of crowds and commercialism, being bypassed by tourists making a beeline for Italy's more famous destinations. Easily accessed from the lakes, they make ideal destinations for day trips.

**Stresa's Heyday**
An elegant haunt of European aristocracy in the 19th century, Stresa became a tourist resort after the tunnelling of the Simplon Pass. Built in 1906, this allowed a railway from the other side of the Alps, giving Stresa instant access.

**Below:** enjoying the warm climate of Limone Sul Garda.

# FOOD AND DRINK

*The local cuisine, often enhanced by a mesmerising waterfront setting, is one of the great joys of travelling around the lakes. Regional dishes range from smoked hams and seasoned sausages to creamy risottos and fresh lake fish.*

## REGIONAL COOKING

Lombard cuisine is highly varied, with ingredients sourced from lakes, mountains and flatlands. Unlike most other regions of Italy, the locals prefer their food rich and creamy. Rice, rather than pasta, is the mainstay of their diet; it is grown on the paddy fields of the Po Valley. Cream is common, and butter prevails over olive oil in local cooking. Lombardy also produces large quantities of corn, which is made into ubiquitous polenta. However, the lighter ingredients of the much-acclaimed Mediterranean diet are also here: abundant fish, fresh fruit and vegetables – plus, of course, a glass or two of red wine.

Each region has its specialities. The Alpine influence can be seen in the array of cheeses, salami, polenta and mushroom dishes on offer in rural inns. The Austrian legacy around the north of Lake Garda has left the locals with a taste for veal, pork, beef, dumplings and gnocchi, while on the southern shore you will find roasts, stews, game and white truffles. Olive oil, oranges, lemons, peaches and pears represent a Mediterranean input. Milan may be moving towards more international tastes, such as sushi, but it still produces the famous *risotto alla milanese*.

## PLACES TO EAT

The region is liberally endowed with restaurants, from simple tavernas to temples of gastronomy. Traditionally, a *ristorante* is smarter and more expensive than a *trattoria*, but these days there is little difference between the two. A simple homely *trattoria* with no menu may serve the most authentic and satisfying fare; there are also elaborate, expensive *trattorie* with international, tourist-focused menus. Likewise an *osteria*, which used to refer only to a simple inn or tavern offering rustic fare, can these days be a chic Michelin-starred restaurant.

### Pizzerias

As with the rest of Italy, the lakes region has a proliferation of inexpensive, unpretentious *pizzerie*, many of them offering pasta, meat and fish as well. The best use wood-fired ovens *(forno a legna)*, but these are sometimes open only in the evening. You can often find places serving cheap slices of pizza *(al taglio)*, the favourite Italian takeaway.

### Cafés and Bars

Cafés are generally referred to in Italian as *bar*, which is actually the counter where coffees are served. They are a way of life for Italians, from the

**Above:** *osso buco,* veal shank stew; salami for sale at a market reflects an Alpine influence.

**Trentino Logo**
When in Trentino, keep an eye out for the 'Osteria Tipica Trentina' signs, indicating restaurants that only serve seasonal local cuisine. These have to offer at least five Trentino cheeses, as well as local wines, grappa and mineral water.

breakfast *cappuccino* and *cornetto* to the lunchtime snack and coffee to the evening *aperitivo* – or, indeed, any type of drink at any time of day. Along with wines and often a remarkable range of cocktails and liqueurs, bars serve filled bread rolls *(panini)*, crustless sandwiches *(tramezzini)* and other snacks. Standing at the bar *(al banco)* is invariably cheaper than sitting at a table with waiter service. You will generally need to pay first and bring the *scontrino* (receipt) to the bar before ordering.

An *enoteca* (wine bar) will offer a plate of sliced *proscuitto crudo*, salamis or cheeses to accompany its wide choice of fine wines.

## UPMARKET DINING

You only have to see all the stars studded across the region's maps in the red Italy Michelin guide to realise just how many gourmet restaurants there are here. The settings can be grandiose or minimalist, the food traditional or innovative. Gualtiero Marchesi, Italy's leading chef and the first to be awarded three Michelin stars, moved his restaurant in Milan to a villa in the Franciacorta region *(see p.79)* in 1993. Renowned for miniature works of art, his signature dish is *riso, oro e zafferono*, saffron rice topped with a sheet of 24-carat gold leaf.

To rub shoulders with celebrities, though not over Michelin-starred cuisine, head to Nobu at the Armani emporium in Milan *(see p.99)*, Il Gatto Nero on Lake Como *(see p.119)* or the Locanda dell'Isola Comacina *(see p.65)*.

## ORDERING YOUR MEAL

Restaurant menus offer four courses: *antipasto*, the starter; *primo*, the first course, which is pasta, risotto or soup; *secondo*, the second course, such as fish or meat (accompanied perhaps by a *contorno*, a vegetable side dish); and finally the *dolce* (dessert), or cheese and coffee. Don't feel pressurised into wading through all four courses; opting for just a couple – and not necessarily the *secondo* – is perfectly acceptable.

Above from far left: harbourside restaurant at Lasize by Lake Garda; fresh local mushrooms; red wine from the Garda region; lakeside café.

## Prices and Menus

Menus at lunchtime are often cheaper than those offered in the evening. Restaurant bills will usually include €1–5 per person for bread and cover charge *(coperto)* and sometimes a 10–15 per cent service charge. If service is not included it is normal to leave a tip. Restaurant prices at the top end of the scale can vary tremendously. At the really prestigious places you won't see much change from €100 per person – and that's without the wine! Set menus vary from a basic two- or three-course meal to a seven or more course blow-out *menu degustazione* (a taster menu), which, if you are feeling flush, is a good way of trying out several of the restaurant's specialities. All set menus include service and cover charge, and some include house wine, mineral water or coffee. 'Tourist menus', usually translated into several languages, are best avoided.

**Above from left:**
dining out in Milan's
Brera neighbourhood;
mountain cheese;
grape lights in Bardo-
lino, where a notable
red wine is produced;
cakes aplenty in a
local *pasticceria.*

## WHAT TO EAT

### Regional Risotto and Ravioli

Thanks to the extensive rice fields on
the Padua plain, risottos are abundant.
Most famous of all, and served
throughout the region, is *risotto alla
milanese*, made with short-grain Arborio
rice, slowly cooked with onions, beef
marrow and stock, served with liberal
amounts of butter and Parmesan cheese,
and flavoured and coloured with saffron.
Rice dishes can be enriched with fish,
seafood, meat, wild *porcini* mushrooms,
truffles or seasonal vegetables.

The other predominant *primo* is ravioli, stuffed perhaps with perch and
parsley, black truffle, or robiola cheese
and basil. Look out for *cansonsèi* ravioli
from the Bergamo region, or *tortelli di
zucca* from Mantua, which is a sweet-
and-sour pasta wrapped around puréed
pumpkin and crushed amaretti, served
with melted butter and grated Parmesan.

### Lake Fish

**Below:** lake fish
drying in the sun.

Lake fish is plentiful and served in a
wide variety of ways. As an *antipasto*,
it may come marinated, smoked,
soused or puréed, as a *primo* it is added
to pasta and risottos, and as a *secondo* it
may be stuffed with vegetables and
herbs, cooked in a sauce, or simply
grilled, fried or baked.

The most commonly found species
are *lavarello*, a white lake fish, perch
*(persico)*, trout *(trota)*, pike *(luccio)* and
char *(salmerino)*. Lake Iseo's specialities are *tinca ripiena*, baked tench
stuffed with breadcrumbs, Parmesan
and parsley and served with polenta,
and *coregone in crosta*, a white fish
flavoured with fennel and cooked in
a salt crust. Around lakes Iseo and
Como restaurant menus may feature
*missultini* (or *missultitt*); this is twaite
shad which has been stretched out on
racks to dry in the sun, then grilled and
served with olive oil and vinegar. On
Lake Garda look out for the highly
prized *carpione*, a type of carp.

### Meat

Although fish is king around the lakes,
most menus also offer a selection of
meat dishes. Along with simply cooked
steak, pork, chicken or veal, you will
find dishes of more humble origin,
such as braised donkey, stewed tripe or,
on the Padua plain, frogs' legs, eels and
snails. The main Milanese specialities
are *osso buco* (veal shank stew), *costoletta
alla milanese* (veal cutlet fried in breadcrumbs) and *cassoeula* (pork and
cabbage casserole). Game features in
the more mountainous regions, and in
Trentino you will find Austrian-style
sausages and sauerkraut, smoked hams
and *speck*.

## Cheese

The region excels in delicious cheeses, from tangy gorgonzola and pungent taleggio to creamy stracchino, robiola and mascarpone. Parmesan-like Grana Padano, produced on the Padua plain, can be eaten sliced as an appetiser or part of a cheese platter, and is used in many pasta and risotto recipes. Market stalls have dozens of regional cheeses, marked either *freschi* (fresh) or *stagionati* (mature). If in doubt, sample a cheese or two before making a purchase.

## WHAT TO DRINK

### Wine and Liqueurs

The DOC *(denominazione di origine controllata)* is an official mark of quality, but don't ignore the *vino da tavola* (house wine), which is often a good local wine. In more sophisticated establishments you will be handed a hefty tome of wines, predominantly regional and national, but international too. Neighbouring Piedmont, Emilia-Romagna and the Veneto, all of which produce larger quantities of wine than Lombardy, will feature on most wine lists.

Although not one of Italy's great wine-producing regions, Lombardy has half a dozen wine regions, and over a quarter of the wine is DOC. The best of the red wine is produced on the steep slopes of the Valtellina in northern Lombardy: Grumello, Inferno, Sassella and Valgella. Franciacorta, south of Lake Iseo, produces reds and still whites, but is best-known for its delicious champagne-style spumante, made from Pinot and Chardonnay grapes.

This is often drunk with fish in local restaurants as well as an *aperitivo*. From the shores of Lake Garda come the dry white Bianco di Custoza and the light, scented red and rosé Bardolinos.

A good meal is usually concluded with a *digestivo* (liqueur), such as a brandy, grappa or limoncello (made from lemons). If you are lucky, this will be on the house.

### Coffee

If you want a small black coffee, ask for a *caffè*, or for a milky coffee, a *caffè latte* (ask for a 'latte' and you will probably get a glass of milk). This and *cappuccino* (or *cappuccio* as the locals call it) are only drunk at breakfast in Italy, although Italians are used to tourists asking for it at all times of day. A good halfway house is a *caffè macchiato*, an espresso with a dash of frothy milk in a small cup. If you want something with a real kick, order a *caffè doppio*, a double espresso; or after a meal, try a *caffè corretto*, with grappa, brandy or Sambuca added. For a good night's sleep forget the real thing and order a *caffè decaffeinato* or *decaff*.

### Dessert

Dessert *(dolce)* is typically an almond or apple tart, or a cake, especially *tiramisù*, the alcoholic chocolate and coffee gateau from the Veneto. Alternatively, you may prefer to do as the Italians and buy an ice cream from the local *gelateria* (there is one on almost every corner), enjoying it while strolling down the street. After all, the Italians are said to make the best ice cream in the world.

**Below:** pick yourself up with an espresso and *biscotto*.

# SHOPPING

*The fact that most Italians now use the expression 'fare lo shopping' might suggest a globalisation of the shopping scene. But the advent of shopping malls (centri commerciali) has barely dented the popularity of small boutiques, gourmet food shops and weekly markets.*

Style and elegance are reflected in the chic stores of Milan, the world's fashion powerhouse, and, to a lesser extent, in smaller cities such as Brescia, Como ('City of Silk') and Bergamo. The lakeside towns and villages offer less choice and higher prices, but an altogether more relaxed shopping experience.

## FOOD AND DRINK

Small food shops throughout the lakes region display a wide variety of tempting delicacies, from home-cured hams and handmade pastas to herbs and honey to local wines and liqueurs. Milan's temple of deli gastronomy is legendary Peck (Via Spadari 9; www. peck.it), a stunning showcase of cheeses, hams, truffles and foie gras. The shores of Lake Garda offer homespun aromatic olive oil, Bardolino wines and Limoncello liqueur made from locally grown lemons, while the wine-growing Franciacorta region produces the best fizz in Italy.

**Below:** cured ham on sale at a weekly open-air market.

## MARKETS

Weekly markets are colourful open-air affairs, with stalls selling flowers, food, fashions, household goods and much more besides. Every Wednesday

Luino on Lake Maggiore hosts what it claims to be the biggest weekly market in Europe (350 or so stalls), with bargain-hunters descending from Switzerland, Austria and Germany as well as Italy. Monthly antiques markets are a source of local handicrafts, although genuine bargains are rare. Nevertheless, bargaining, even if only in sign language, is always worth a try.

## FASHION IN MILAN

Since the 1980s Milan has been a world centre for fashion design, drawing huge numbers of visitors – many celebrities among them – to the fashion fairs and the flagship stores of Armani, Prada and other top designers. At the opening of the fairs, the international paparazzi descend on the city, while the hip hotels and stylish restaurants are packed with celebrities and supermodels.

The flagship outlets of the big designer names are conveniently concentrated in a small, attractive area, known as the Quadrilatero d'Oro (Golden Quadrangle; *see p. 98*). Stores range from chic little shops resembling art galleries, to modern emporia such as Armani, complete with restaurant, bookstore, flower shop and furnishings, as well as fashions.

Prices are not for the faint-hearted, but if your credit card can't stretch to cutting-edge collections, there are plenty of more affordable fashions in the city centre, as well as the arty and ethnic boutiques of the Brera and Ticinese quarters.

## COMO SILK

Como, centre of Italy's silk industry, has produced silk and other textiles since the 15th century. Silkworms are no long longer bred here, but Chinese fibres are imported to be woven, dyed and printed. Armani, Hermès and Versace are just three of the famous designers who depend on Como for their silk. The Como tourist office (Piazza Cavour 17) provides a list of factory outlets, some offering as much as 40–70 per cent discounts.

*Factory Outlets*
The lakes region has a large number of *spacci* (discount factory outlets), selling seductive clothes, cult-design icons, crafts, leatherware and gourmet gifts. For full immersion into the art of silk, visit Como's La Tessitura at Viale Roosevelt 2 (www.mantero.com), a huge, spectacularly converted late-19th-century factory. Multimedia displays describe silk-making processes, fashion trends and the products of silk manufacturer Mantero – supplier to Yves Saint Laurent, Calvin Klein and other big names – which are on sale here. Frey Emporio della Seta in Fino Mornasco (Via Risorgimento 9; www.frey.it), southwest of Como,

sells silk ties, scarves and garments of top designers. The functional but well-designed Franciacorta Outlet Village (Rodengo Saiano, 7km/4½ miles west of Brescia) has 160 stores and is a good choice if you are visiting the wine estates in the area *(see p.77)*. When in Bellagio, be sure to visit Pierangelo Masciadri's silk shop at Salita Mella 19 *(see p.56)*.

## SHOPPING IN BERGAMO

In the heart of the region, Bergamo is a delightful city for shopping as well as sightseeing. The choice is not huge, but the upper town has some lovely food shops and clothes boutiques, while Il Sentierone and Via XX Settembre in the lower town have fashions, silk, leather goods and jewellery. La Rinascente department store on Via XX Settembre is part of a stylish Milanese chain, selling high-end clothes, accessories and domestic goods. A shuttle bus service links the upper and lower towns with the airport just 5km (3 miles) away.

**Above from far left:** shopping arcade in Bellagio; silk ties from Como; shoe shop in Salò.

**Shopping Hours**
Most shops are open Mon–Sat 8am–7pm, closing around 1–4pm. In larger towns some shops and department stores stay open all day and have limited Sunday opening. Food markets are weekly, antiques markets are monthly. Local tourist offices will have details.

**Left:** Prada boutique in Milan's Galleria Vittorio Emanuele II.

# ENTERTAINMENT

*The lakeside towns and villages tend to be peaceful places by night, favouring leisurely dinners, lakeside strolls and a liqueur at the local bar. But entertainment is never too far away, whether it is the nightclubs of Brescia and Bergamo, the opera or hip bars of Milan, or the Gardaland theme park.*

The Lombardy region has a strong musical tradition. Violinmaker Stradivarius and composer Monteverdi both came from Cremona, Donizetti was born and died in Bergamo, and Verdi composed *La Traviata* while staying on Lake Como. Today opera, concerts and music festivals take place in cities across the region and in castles, villas and other historic locations around the lakes.

## FESTIVALS AND EVENTS

The lakes and Lombard cities stage some of the finest events on the Italian cultural calendar. Events take place all year round, and include classical music festivals, boat processions, food and wine fairs, fireworks over the lake and jazz extravaganzas. The most prestigious event of the lakes is Stresa's Settimane Musicali (www.stresafestival. eu), a spring-to-autumn festival of classical concerts featuring internationally renowned musicians, performed in churches and other historical venues around Lake Maggiore.

Brescia plays host to a piano festival in May and June, and Gardone Riviera on Lake Garda presents drama, opera and concerts in the open-air theatre of the Vittoriale

degli Italiani in July and August. The tiny wine-producing region of Franciacorta south of Lake Iseo stages a sparkling wine and food festival in September, along with wine- and food-tasting events in the vineyards at weekends (www.stradadelfranciacorta. it). The Grape and Wine Festival at Bardolino on Lake Garda is another cork-popping event held in the autumn. This is the time to buy quantities of wine very cheaply.

### Festival of San Giovanni

One of the most ancient and magical lake festivals is that of San Giovanni (St John), celebrated at Isola Comacina, Lake Como, on the weekend closest to St John the Baptist's Day (24 June). Mass is held in the church ruins, and thousands of bobbing boats are illuminated by candles and fireworks. For some of the best views, you can join a night cruise with onboard dinner and dancing (see www.navigazionelaghi.it for details).

## NIGHTLIFE

Milan apart, the region is not renowned for discos and nightclubs. Garda is the liveliest of the lakes, particularly in the town of Desenzano del Garda, where

**Opera in Verona**
If you are staying on the south or east side of Lake Garda, try to take in an opera extravaganza in nearby Verona's great Roman amphitheatre. The experience is an unforgettable one, and you don't have to be an opera buff to enjoy it. The lavish, open-air performances take place from late June to the end of August and the operas alternate, so that during one month you have a choice of at least four different performances. Book well in advance on www.arena.it or by telephoning the call centre on 045-800 5151 (tickets range from €24–200).

bars, live music and nightclubs attract a younger crowd. Como, although not exactly a hot spot, has some sociable late-opening bars along the Lungo Lario Trieste waterfront.

Brescia is lively after dark, especially at weekends. You can enjoy concerts and opera at the Teatro Grande, or live it up at late-night bars or discos. Bergamo offers upmarket wining and dining, classical concerts and plenty of bars, but for nightclubs you need to head out of town.

## Milan

Milan offers the most vibrant nightlife in Italy, with a huge range of classical concerts, theatre, live jazz and rock, pop concerts and scores of stylish bars and nightclubs. It is also home to La Scala (tel: 02-88791; www.teatroalla scala.org), one of the world's most prestigious opera houses *(see also p.98)*.

To find details of clubs, pubs and trendsetting cocktail bars in Milan check out the excellent website www. ciaomilano.it. Another useful source of information is *Hello Milano* magazine (www.hellomilano.it), which gives the month's listings of everything from street markets and festivals to films in English, opera and dance perform- ances, concerts and live rock.

## FAMILY ENTERTAINMENT

There is plenty to keep youngsters entertained on the lakes, from boat trips and cable-car rides to leisure parks and castles. Lake Garda is by far the best-equipped lake for families,

with vast theme parks, water parks and sandy beaches. Concentrated in a 25km (15½-mile) radius in the south- east of Lake Garda, there are no fewer than six major attractions.

### Theme Parks

Thousands of holidaymakers descend annually to the shore north of Pesch- iera del Garda, home to Gardaland (www.gardaland.it), Italy's number one theme park. It boasts over 40 attrac- tions and 40 shows, plus the brand new Gardaland Sea Life (www.sealife europe.com). Situated 4km (2½ miles) to the north is Canevaworld (www. canevaworld.it), which comprises Aquaparadise, Europe's biggest water park; Movieland, dedicated to the film world; and Medieval Times, a show with dinner and medieval jousting. Further up the coast, the modern funicular at Malcesine, with rotating panoramic cable-cars, is a great way of getting up to the mountain ridge of Monte Baldo *(see p.87)*.

### Water Parks and Gardens

The Parco Cavour near Valeggio sul Mincio (www.parcoacquaticocavour.it) and Parco Picoverde at Custoza (www. picoverde.it) provide plenty of aquatic entertainment. Nature lovers should head for the Parco Natura Viva at Bus- solengo (www.parconaturaviva.it), a centre for the protection of animals at risk of extinction. The Parco Giardino Sigurtà (www.sigurta.it) at Valeggio sul Mincio features gorgeous gardens, with 18 fish-filled ponds, a toy railway and nature trails.

**Above from far left:** Gardaland theme park; La Scala; Salò by night.

**Villa Pallavicino** Lake Maggiore's Stresa *(see p.32)* may be a rather sedate resort, but children can be kept enter- tained by ferry rides, the Monte Mottarone cable-car and a visit to Villa Pallavicino (www. parcozoopallavicino.it). The extensive gardens are home to animals, exotic birds and a children's playground. In summer a mini-train provides a shuttle ser- vice between the park and Stresa's centre.

**Below:** animals at Parco Natura Viva.

# SPORTS AND OUTDOOR ACTIVITIES

*Lakes, mountains and wind lend themselves to myriad year-round sporting activities. Lake Garda is a sporting paradise, boasting wind-surfing, sailing, hiking and cycling, while at Ascona on Lake Maggiore you can ski in the morning and play a round of golf in the afternoon.*

**Activities on Como**
To take the effort out of arranging your own sports on Lake Como, contact the Cavalcario Club (www.bellagio-mountains.it), which organises mountain-biking tours, trekking, paragliding and horse-riding in the mountains around Bellagio.

**Football**
Italians are mad about *calcio* (football), and particularly since their victory in the World Cup in 2006. The two top teams, Internazionale and AC Milan, draw huge crowds to Milan's stadium. The teams play on alternative Sundays from September to May. For tickets visit www.acmilan.com and www.inter.it.

Sailors and windsurfers from all over Europe descend on the northern shores of Lake Garda, where constant winds fill the sails all year round. The *pelèr* (or *suer*) wind blows from the north in the morning, while the *ora* from the south starts in the early afternoon and lasts until the evening.

Alpine foothills offer wonderful trekking and mountaineering, and mountain bikers are increasingly lured by the quiet paths and breathtaking views above the lakes. Golf is popular too, with fine courses around Francia-corta and Lake Garda, and the oldest course in Italy above Lake Como.

## WATERSPORTS

Lake Garda has countless sailing regattas, both local and international, including world championships. Riva del Garda and Torbole in the north have numerous watersports schools with gear to rent and tuition for all levels. For children and beginners, the resorts slightly further south with more sheltered bays and gentler winds, such as Val di Sogno, are more suitable (see www.stickl.com). Water-skiers are more restricted, as motorboats are banned

from the northern section of the lake and other popular windsurfing areas.

On Lake Maggiore, Laveno, Luino, Ascona and Locarno are bases for sailing and windsurfing. On Lake Como the town of Como offers opportunities for sailing, water-skiing, diving and canoeing, while further up the lake at Menaggio and Bellagio you can water-ski and hire a motorboat.

## HIKING AND CLIMBING

Trekking has become enormously popular. Ridges above the lakes, wood-land trails and the Alpine mountains provide wonderful scenery and cater for all levels of fitness, from easygoing hikes to strenuous mountain-climbing.

On Lake Garda the Monte Baldo ridge has well-marked trails and glor-ious views, as does Monte Mottarone above Lake Maggiore. Both have cable-car access (from Stresa and Mal-cesine respectively).

For hikes in the Alps, the best months are May to October. The Club Alpino Italiano or CAI (Italian Alpine Club; www.caimilano.it – Italian only) organises guided tours, provides maps and runs shelters for serious hikers.

Many of the routes are not as well marked or developed as in other European countries, and for serious hiking you may want to hire one of their local guides.

## CYCLING AND MOUNTAIN BIKING

Cycling in the region is a serious pursuit. Lombardy alone has nearly 700 cycling clubs and 1,200 annual races. The steep slopes around the lakes are popular with mountain bikers, and the Riva del Garda bike festival in spring attracts top cycling celebrities. For a thrilling ride down a mountain without the uphill struggle, take a bike on the cable-car up to Monte Baldo or Monte Mottarone – or hire one at the top.

## GOLF

Lakes Maggiore, Como and Garda have golf courses, many of them with wonderful views of the lakes and Alps. Some of the finest courses are around Franciacorta and Lake Garda: the Franciacorta Golf Club (tel: 030-984 167; www.franciacortagolfclub.it) is to the south of Lake Iseo, while Palazzo Arzaga (tel: 030-680 600; www.palazzo arzaga.it) and Garda Golf (www.garda golf.it) are both to the west of Lake Garda between Salò and Desenzano del Garda. The oldest club is the Menaggio and Cadennabia Golf Club (www.menaggio.it) at Lake Como, which was set up by four Englishmen around a century ago. Another prestigious and long-established location is the Villa d'Este Golf Club (tel: 031-200 200; www.villadeste.com).

## EXTREME SPORTS

Paragliding is popular on Monte Baldo, Monte Maddalena near Brescia, and from Bellagio (Cavalcalario Club; www. bellagio-mountains.it). Lake Garda's winds are ideal for kitesurfing. The Stickl Sportscamp organises courses for all levels, communicating with kite-surfers through radio receivers fitted into the helmets. If you wish to leap head first down a ravine, try bungee-jumping at Verzasca (220m/720ft) and Centovalli (70m/220ft) in Swiss Ticino.

## ROCK-CLIMBING

The northern end of Lake Garda, where walls rise to 1,200m (3,900ft), is a haven for rock-climbers. Arco, just north of Torbole, has Europe's largest open-air wall and hosts the Rockmaster free-climbing world championships in September. For climbing at all levels check out www.alpineguide.com.

## SKIING

For guaranteed snow you have to head as far north as Bormio, the mountain resort that hosted the World Ski Championships in 2005. Snow permitting, you can also ski and snowboard at Monte Baldo on Lake Garda, Monte Mottarone and Macugnaga on Lake Maggiore, the Grigna mountains above Lecco on Lake Como, and the resorts above Bergamo and Brescia.

**Above from far left:** Lake Garda is a prime location for sailing, particularly in the north; rowing on Lake Varese.

**Cyclists' Sanctuary**
The steep hill of the Madonna del Ghisallo (12km/7½ miles south of Bellagio) serves as a challenging last lap of a number of national and local cycling races. Thousands of cyclists and visitors come here annually – and not just for the panoramic views of Lake Como. At the top of the hill is a church dedicated to the Madonna del Ghisallo, who in 1949 was declared the patroness of cyclists by official papal edict. The church then became a cycling museum, displaying bikes and equipment of cycling champions, historic models, trophies and other memorabilia. In 2006 the state-of-the-art three-storey Museo di Ciclismo (Cycling Museum; www. museodelghisallo.it) opened beside the church to house some of the exhibits.

# HISTORY: KEY DATES

*The lakes' proximity to the great trade routes between the Mediterranean and Central Europe played a key role, ensuring prosperity, but also enticing a succession of foreign invaders. Each new arrival made its mark, contributing a rich history and culture to this beautiful region.*

## EARLY HISTORY

| | |
|---|---|
| **8,000BC** | Emergence of the Valle Camonica civilisation, with the first rocks carved by Camuni tribes. |
| **202–191BC** | Romans start to establish colonies in Milan, Como, Brescia, Verona and other settlements. |
| **222BC** | Romans conquer Milan. |
| **AD313** | Emperor Constantine grants freedom of worship to Christians in the Edict of Milan. |
| **4th century** | Milan becomes the de facto capital of the western Roman empire. |
| **568** | The Lombards establish their capital at Pavia. |

## THE MIDDLE AGES

| | |
|---|---|
| **774** | Charlemagne takes the Lombard crown. |
| **1024** | Emergence of the *comuni*, or independent city states. |
| **1118–27** | Como defeated by Milan in the Ten Years War. |
| **1152** | The German prince Frederick Barbarossa is named Holy Roman Emperor. |
| **1260–1387** | Lake Garda and Verona ruled by the Scaligeri (della Scala) dynasty. |
| **1277–1447** | Duchy of Milan ruled by the Visconti dynasty. |
| **1347–8** | The Black Death devastates the population of northern Italy. |
| **1405** | Venetians conquer Verona, Padua and Bergamo. |
| **1450–99** | Duchy of Milan ruled by the Sforza dynasty. |

**Roman Buildings**
The greatest architectural legacies of Roman rule in the region are Sirmione's Grottoes of Catullus – a Roman villa traditionally believed to have belonged to the poet *(see p.82)* – Brescia's Capitoline Temple *(pictured top)* and Verona's amphitheatre *(bottom)* – one of the largest and finest surviving from ancient times.

## FOREIGN INTERVENTION

| | |
|---|---|
| **1530** | Charles V is crowned Holy Roman Emperor and Lombardy comes under his rule. |
| **1714** | Spain cedes Lombardy to the Austrian (Habsburg) empire. |
| **1796** | Napoleon invades northern Italy. |
| **1814–70** | The Risorgimento – a movement for the liberation and political unification of Italy. |

| 1848 | The Milanese rebel against the Austrians, who re-enter the city. |
| 1859 | France defeats Austria at the battles of Magenta and Solferino. |
| 1861 | Italy is unified under Vittorio Emanuele II, first king of Italy. |
| 1871 | Italian unification. |

## 20TH CENTURY

| 1915 | Italy joins the World War I Allies. |
| 1922 | Mussolini seizes power in Italy. |
| 1940 | Italy enters World War II as an ally of Nazi Germany. |
| 1943–5 | Italy surrenders to the Allies; Mussolini is installed in the Republic of Salò. |
| 1945 | Mussolini and his mistress, Claretta Petacci, are captured by partisans and executed. |
| 1951 | Italy joins the EEC, forerunner of the European Union (EU). |
| 1992 | Tangentopoli ('Bribesville') corruption scandals rock the north and lead to an overhaul of public life. |
| 1994 | Emergence of Forza Italia, a right-wing political party led by media tycoon Silvio Berlusconi. |

## 21ST CENTURY

| 2001 | Silvio Berlusconi is elected prime minister. |
| 2002 | The euro replaces the lira as the official Italian currency. |
| 2006 | Romano Prodi's centre-left coalition narrowly defeats Silvio Berlusconi in the general election. Italy wins FIFA World Cup. |
| 2008 | Silvio Berlusconi's People of Freedom Alliance defeats the Democrats in the general election. |

**Above from far left:**
Battle of Solferino in 1859; a steamer on Lake Como.

**Silvio Berlusconi**
Despite questions over his personal probity and stranglehold over the media, Silvio Berlusconi won a decisive victory in April 2008, marking his third term in office and the 62nd Italian government since World War II. The 71-year-old right-wing politician heads the People of Freedom Alliance (PDL), a merger of his Forza Italia party with the National Alliance and other conservative parties. His main task now is to revive Italy's ailing economy.

GRAND HÔTEL
# TREMEZZO

**Left:** vintage tourist poster for the classic hotel on Lake Como (*see p.114*).

# WALKS AND TOURS

# 1

# THE BORROMEAN ISLANDS

*An island-hopping day trip from the belle époque resort of Stresa to Isola Bella, Isola dei Pescatori and Isola Madre at the centre of Lake Maggiore. Explore the villas and grounds of these three small exotic outcrops, lunching in a rustic fish restaurant on Isola dei Pescatori.*

## Shuttle Service

A new shuttle service offers departures to Isola Bella and Isola dei Pescatori from Carciano, northwest of the centre of Stresa, departing near the Mottarone cable car. You can leave the car in the large parking lot near the ticket office. A mid-morning ferry will give you time to visit the house and gardens on Isola Bella and have lunch on Isola dei Pescatori, before returning to Carciano in the mid-afternoon.

**Below:** peacocks perambulate the gardens of Isola Bella.

---

**DISTANCE** 13km (8 miles) return trip by ferry
**TIME** A full day
**START/END** Stresa
**POINTS TO NOTE**

Regular ferries operate from Stresa to the islands. Pick up a timetable from the ferry station or check times on www.navigazionelaghi.it. If you do not want the restrictions of a timetable, consider taking one of the not-too-extortionate private boats beside the ferry station. The ferry service stops in the early evening, but if you wish to dine on the Isola dei Pescatori, both the Verbano and Belvedere restaurants offer a free boat service. Be sure to reserve a table for lunch or dinner.

The islands are packed throughout the season; make an early start if you want to see all three islands in a day and avoid the worst of the crowds.

---

## Lake Maggiore

Despite its name, Lake Maggiore is the second-largest Italian lake after Garda. The long and narrow ribbon of water stretches 65km (40 miles) and is bordered by Lombardy to the east,

Piedmont to the west and the Swiss canton of Ticino to the north. The scenery varies from the wild northern mountainous, where the Swiss pre-Alps descend towards the lake, to the gentler Mediterranean-like shores of the south. The jewel-like Borromean Islands lie in the scenic centre of the lake.

## The Islands

Located off the shore of Stresa *(see p.32)*, the Borromean Islands bask in the warmth of a Mediterranean micro-climate. Even though these lovely outcrops constitute the most popular excursion in the lakes, they retain a languid charm. Henry James described 'the delicious old Borromean Islands' as 'a quaint mixture of tawdry flummery and genuine beauty, a sort of tropical half-splendid, half-slovenly Little Trianon and Hampton Court'. In those days tourists were rowed to the islands by hotel lackeys; today they depend on the bustling ferry crossing.

## Catching the Ferry

At the ferry station on Piazza Marconi, beside the tourist office, buy a ticket that includes entrances to the island sights. Alight at the first stop – Isola Bella.

## ISOLA BELLA

Whereas Isola dei Pescatori was styled as a rural retreat and Isola Madre as an enchanted garden, **Isola Bella** ❶ (tel: 0323-30556; www.borromeo turismo.it; mid-Mar–mid-Oct daily 9am–5.30pm; charge) was always intended to be a showy pleasure palace. In recent times Isola Bella has served as the Borromean princes' summer residence; the family stays in the island palace *(see margin, p.30)*. To protect the family's privacy, and its art collection, two-thirds of the palace is closed to the public, but it is still worth seeing, not least for the beguiling Baroque gardens and the palatial treasures on show.

### From a Rock to a Monument
Although Isola Bella began as little more than a rocky islet with a view, over the course of centuries it became a delightful folly. In the 1620s Count Carlo III Borromeo was inspired to create a full-blown monument to his wife Isabella. To realise his vision the rocks were transformed into an island with 10 terraces designed to resemble the prow of a ship in full sail. Boatloads of soil were transported to this barren island, as well as Baroque statuary and the building materials needed for the creation of a palatial villa. The works continued under his son, Vitiliano VI, and were virtually complete by the time of his death in 1670. Even so, inspired by the original plans, family descendants continued to embellish the island until the 1950s when Vitiliano IX, the last member of the family to attempt

major modifications, died before building his cherished harbour.

### Borromean Palace
The island creates a dramatic impact as you approach. Disembarking from the ferry, follow the flow to the turreted **Palazzo Borromeo**. The stern façade belies a lavish interior, full of gilt and stucco-work, marble statues and Murano chandeliers. The palace's high-ceilinged rooms contain a fine collection of 16th- to 18th-century northern Italian art, though it is encrusted in a Baroque clutter of stucco-work and heraldic crests, only partially redeemed by bold flourishes such as a cantilevered spiral staircase. Lavishly overstuffed public rooms connect a gilded throne room, an empire-style ballroom and a Flemish long gallery housing tapestries emblazoned with the unicorns that adorn the dynasty's distinctive crest.

**Above from far left:**
Isola Bella; view of Lake Maggiore and the three Borromean Islands from the Botanical Garden above Stresa *(see p.36)*.

**Ticket Tip**
Note that you can buy a combined entry ticket for both Isola Bella and Isola Madre from either island; it is cheaper than paying separately to visit each island.

## A Powerful Dynasty

Lake Maggiore was a fiefdom of the noble Borromei clan in the 15th century, and the family has succeeded in holding onto some of the most beautiful parts, not least the Borromean Islands. This powerful Milanese dynasty has produced patrons of education, religious reformers, cardinals, popes and even a saint, San Carlo. The family scions are still fabulously wealthy owners of palaces in Milan and priceless art collections. These days they also receive the revenue from toll roads and fishing rights over the lake.

**Below:** statuary in the Baroque gardens of Palazzo Borromeo.

### Napoleon Slept Here

The palace has witnessed numerous momentous historical events, and has played host to emperors and statesmen. In 1797 Napoleon slept in one of the bedrooms – a ponderous neoclassical chamber decorated in what was the politically correct Directoire style. The ornate music room was the setting for the Stresa peace conference of 1935: it was here that Italy, Britain and France failed to agree on a strategic response to Hitler's programme of rapid re-armament, a missed opportunity that hastened the momentum towards war.

### Grottoes and Caverns

Designed as a cool summer retreat, the mysterious area beneath the palace conceals bizarre artificial **grottoes**, with tufa-stone walls studded with shells, pebbles and fossils. The maritime mood is sustained in the statue of a coolly reclining nude and caverns dotted with marine imagery. This grotesque creation reflects the contemporary taste

for *Wunderkammer* – chambers of marvels designed to enchant visitors with their eclectic displays. In the case of Isola Bella, however, the greatest marvel lies outside.

### Gardens and Terraces

The Baroque **gardens** envelop the palace in sweeping arcs, with dramatic architectural perspectives accentuated by grandiose urns, obelisks, fountains and statues. Although the terraced gardens abound in shady arbours, whimsical water features and mannered statuary, the sum is greater than its parts. Serried ranks of orange and lemon trees meet flower beds before fading into a studied confusion of camellias and magnolias, laurels, cypresses, jasmine and pomegranate.

The ship-shaped **terraces**, crowned by a four-tiered folly studded with shells and topped by cherubs and classical gods, culminate in a huge statue of a heraldic unicorn. It is all rather pompous, but you can't fail to admire the variety of exotic flora, and the sublime views across to Monte Mottarone *(see p.36)*. The pièce de résistance is a shell-shaped **amphi-theatre** that serves as a delightful setting for summer concerts.

After your visit return to the ferry landing stage (the rest of the island is awash with trinket stands and poor-quality tourist restaurants).

## ISOLA DEI PESCATORI

A five-minute ferry ride from Isola Bella brings you to **Isola dei Pescatori ❷**, or

as you hear the ferrymen announce it, 'Isola Superiore dei Pescatori'. The full name derives from the Latin *superior*, indicating that it is further north than Isola Bella (Isola Inferiore).

The island is a pretty fishing village less dedicated to fishing than to the preservation of its film-set picturesque appearance. It is a place for pottering down tiny alleys and peering at the lake, or even paddling off the pebble beach facing Isola Bella. The maze of passageways conjures up the mood of a remote Greek island: a frescoed parish church fades into a view of fishing nets drying in the sun or courtyards of basking cats. Henry James praised this pocket of Italy for making one feel 'out of the rush and crush of the modern world'.

*Lunch Break*

Of the three islands the Isola dei Pescatori is the best bet for lunch, with two inviting waterside restaurants serving fresh fish: the **Hotel Ristorante Verbano**, see ①①, adjoining the pebble beach, or the **Hotel Ristorante Belvedere**, see ①②, five minutes' walk north.

After lunch take the next ferry to Isola Madre, which stops at the resort of Baveno *(see p.38)* en route.

### ISOLA MADRE

Enjoy the cooling breezes on the ferry to **Isola Madre ❸** (tel: 0323-30556; www.borromeoturismo.it; Mar–Oct daily 9am–5.30pm; charge). Here on the largest of the islands, and what was

once the wildest, you will find gently landscaped gardens. The island is home to Europe's largest Kashmiri cypress and some of the first camellias planted in Italy. Best seen in spring, the camellias are part of a patchwork formed by shady paths, ancient cedars, mimosa, magnolias and giant rhododendrons, and populated by white peacocks, Chinese pheasants and parrots. The best time to visit is April for camellias or May for azaleas and rhododendrons.

The 16th-century **villa** – an apparently austere Mannerist affair created as a home rather than a palace – is a bit stifling and gloomy. The Borromean family indulged their love of theatre here – check out the curious collection of puppet theatres, puppets and dolls.

In the evening you could also dine on Isola dei Pescatori – it is at its most romantic when the crowds have gone. Otherwise, return to Stresa, bearing in mind the last ferry departs at around 6.30pm.

Above from far left: Isola dei Pescatori; fountains and terraces at Palazzo Borromeo; dusk falls over Isola Madre.

**Below:** fishing nets on the Isola dei Pescatori.

Food and Drink 🍴

① HOTEL RISTORANTE VERBANO
Via Ugo Ara 2, Isola dei Pescatori; tel: 0323-30408; Apr–Oct; €€
An atmospheric restaurant with a lakeside terrace that is especially fine in the evenings. The fish-based cuisine might be overrated but the setting, overlooking Isola Bella, is hard to beat.

② HOTEL RISTORANTE BELVEDERE
Via di Mezzo, Isola dei Pescatori; tel: 0323-32292; www.belvedere-isolapescatori.it; €
An idyllic waterside setting with meals served in the garden, on the veranda or in the lakeview dining room. The emphasis is on lake fish, such as *lavarello* grilled with butter and sage, trout or perch.

Both restaurants offer a free evening boat service from/to Stresa.

# STRESA AND ANGERA CASTLE

*This tour combines a stroll in Stresa, 'Queen of the Lake', with a cruise of the southern section of Lake Maggiore, alighting at Angera for a leisurely fish lunch and the finest fortress on the lake.*

## Music Festival

Angera's Rocca Borromeo is one of the many venues of the Settimane Music-ale di Stresa (www. stresafestival.eu), the top classical music festival of the region. Founded in 1961, it has expanded from Stresa to towns and villages all around Lake Maggiore. From spring to late summer concerts take place in churches and historic buildings, and on islands. Another venue is the lovely hermitage of Santa Caterina del Sasso *(see p.37).* Events feature the festival's own resident orchestra, as well as renowned inter-national musicians.

**DISTANCE** Walk in Stresa: 3km (2 miles); cruise to Angera and back: 32km (20 miles)

**TIME** A half day or leisurely full day

**START/END** Stresa

**POINTS TO NOTE**

Check ferry times at least a day in advance from the landing stage at Piazza Marconi or from the tourist office next door (tel: 0323-30150). Timetables are also available online at www.navigazionelaghi.it. Boats from Stresa to Angera are spas-modic, but there is always a late morning ferry (taking 50 minutes) and a hydrofoil (20 minutes, but more expensive). The last boats back from Angera leave in the mid-afternoon.

Note that both recommended restaurants in Angera are closed on Mondays.

## STRESA

The main resort on the Piedmontese shore, **Stresa ❶** was a *belle époque* wintering ground, the popularity of which was enhanced by the opening of the Simplon Pass in 1906. A dowager resort distinctly past its prime, Stresa is considered to be the noble part of Lake Maggiore. It found favour with both Queen Victoria and Winston Churchill, and remains popular with superannuated politicians and former world leaders: Margaret Thatcher and Helmut Kohl have both been known to have a soft spot for Stresa. It may have lost the cachet it once enjoyed, but as a base on the lake the resort still can't be beaten for views, excursions and easy access to the Borromean Islands *(see p.28).*

### Lakeside Promenade

From Stresa's bustling waterfront at Piazza Marconi take the **lakeside promenade** northwest towards the sandy Lido and Monte Mottarone cable-car. The main road divides the immaculate garden-lined promenade from the succession of imposing hotels and elegant villas. Replete with beguiling vistas over the Borromean Islands, the lakeside rose gardens have a sedate air that complements the resort's genteel reputation.

The 15-minute stroll towards Baveno passes Stresa's grandest hotels, the sole relic of its *fin de siècle* heyday. The 18th-century **Villa Ducale**, where the

philosopher Antonio Rosmini died in 1855 (and which is now the Rosmini Study Centre) gives way to the Art Nouveau Regina Palace and its renowned restaurant, followed by the **Grand Hotel des Iles Borromées**, where literary luminaries have stayed *(see p.112).* Among them was Ernest Hemingway, who recuperated here after being wounded in battle and then used the resort as a backdrop in *A Farewell to Arms* (1929). At the end of the promenade you come to the Lido and a cable-car which rises up to Monte Mottarone for superb lake views *(see p.36).*

### CRUISE TO ANGERA

Retrace your steps to the landing stage for a ferry to Angera and secure a seat on the right-hand side of the boat. The route hugs the western shore before crossing to the Lombardy side of the lake.

*Sights En Route*

During the cruise you will pass Stresa's neoclassical **Villa Pallavicino**, with landscaped grounds and an appealing zoo *(see margin, p.21)* and the delightful village of **Belgirate**. Further south, towards Arona, are clusters of celebrity villas, especially around **Meina**, where fashion designers such as Armani and Ferre have homes. You might catch tantalising glimpses of neoclassical mansions within parks and gardens that are now home to British super-models and world-class footballers such as striker Alessandro del Piero.

Above from far left: view of Lake Maggiore from above Stresa; angling at dusk.

Below: ferry skipper.

## ANGERA AND ROCCA BORROMEO

In **Angera** the medieval hulk of the **Rocca Borromeo ②** (Via alla Rocca; tel: 0331-931 300; www.roccaborromeo.it; mid-Mar–3rd week Oct 9.30am–5.30pm; charge), dominating the town, soon looms into view. In the 11th century the twin fortresses of Arona and Angera were built to safeguard the strategic southern part of the lake. Arona's fortress was destroyed by Napoleon. Angera's, the best-preserved castle on the lake, became the prop-

erty of the Milanese Visconti in the late 13th century, but in 1450 it passed to the Borromean dynasty, who converted it into a residence and have owned it ever since. The Visconti covered the walls with frescoes celebrating the glory and longevity of their dynasty. The Gothic **Sala di Giustizia** (Hall of Justice), a vaulted chamber, is adorned with signs of the zodiac and scenes of military victories. For spectacular views over the lake take the rickety steps up the **Torre Principale**.

### Doll Museum

A dozen rooms of the castle are devoted to the **Museo della Bambola**, one of the largest collections of dolls in Europe. Dating from the 18th to the 20th century, the dolls are remarkably detailed and varied; they are made of everything from wood and wax to papier mâché, fabric and plastic, and include fat grumpy-faced porcelain dolls that look more like miniature adults than childish toys. The collection also features dolls' furniture, toys, board games and children's clothes from the 18th century, including intricate court costumes. A section dedicated to French and German automatons (1870–1920), all fully functioning, was added in 2002.

### Lunch and a Vista of Arona

For lunch the best options are the restaurant of the **Vecchia Angera** in the Hotel Pavone, see ⑪①, a 10–15-minute walk south from the Rocca Borromeo, or the **Hotel Lido**, see ⑪②, right on the lake.

---

## Food and Drink

**① VECCHIA ANGERA**
Hotel Pavone, Via F. Borromeo 14; tel: 0331-930 224; Tue–Sun; €€
An unpretentious restaurant patronised by locals as well as tourists. The choice of fish depends on availability from the market; the pastas and puddings are all home-made. Typical dishes are ravioli with sea bass and prawns, risotto with *porcini* and Parmesan, fillet steak, perch fillets or tuna with a sesame crust.

**② HOTEL LIDO**
Viale Libertà 11; tel: 0331-930 232; www.hotellido.it; Tue–Sun; €€
A good fish restaurant within a lakeshore hotel. Try the ravioli filled with four types of lake fish, mixed grill of fish, seafood risotto or lake-fish sushi, and select from a list of 300 wines.

**③ LA BOTTE**
Via Mazzini 6/8; tel: 0323-30462; Fri–Wed; €
'The Barrel' is a tiny wood-panelled restaurant in a narrow street just a minute's walk from the main piazza. The owner is also the chef, and both locals and tourists enjoy the warm atmosphere and seasonal specialities, such as local sausages, plus good pastas and pizzas.

**④ LA PIEMONTESE**
Via Mazzini 25; tel: 0323-30235; Tue–Sun; €€€
A long-established Stresa restaurant with a delightful setting and friendly atmosphere. Meals are taken in the cosy dark-wood interior or the vine-covered terrace. Great lake fish, wonderful cheeses, heavenly desserts and choice vintage wines.

This is the narrowest section of Lake Maggiore, and, mists permitting, there should be good views across to **Arona** on the Piedmontese shore. Towering over the town is the **San Carlone** – a colossal statue of the locally born, beatified reformer San Carlo Borromeo (1538–84) – which, when built, was the world's tallest statue after New York's Statue of Liberty *(see feature, below)*.

### BACK TO STRESA

After lunch take the ferry or hydrofoil back to Stresa. On arrival you might want to regain your land legs before going to your hotel or embarking on a dinner cruise. The resort is short of specific sights, but it does possess a certain faded charm, from a tiny harbour full of bobbing fishing boats to the sunny **Piazza Cadorna**, the main inland square which teems with life at night. Sit down under the plane trees and sip a drink in **Caffè Nazionale** or get an ice cream at the neighbouring **Angolo del Gelato**.

This is prime shopping time, so you could saunter down Via Bolognaro to see the old-fashioned shops, or continue to Via Garibaldi, parallel with the lakeshore, which has a reliable pastry shop and a friendly wine bar, **Da Giannino** at no. 32. If planning a picnic for the following day, call in at Stresa's main supermarket, GS, located at Via Roma 11, just off Piazza Cadorna.

For dinner avoid the restaurants on Piazza Cadorna in favour of **La Botte**, see ⑪③, or **La Piemontese**, see ⑪④, both in Via Mazzini, the street linking Piazza Cadorna and Piazza Matteotti.

## San Carlone

The Rocca, like the Borromean Islands off Stresa, belongs to the ubiquitous Borromeo dynasty. A famous member of the family was San Carlo (St Charles), who was born in 1538 in the (now ruined) castle of Arona and devoted his life to the reform and welfare of the Church. A meteoric rise to power saw him become a cardinal at the age of 22 and archbishop of Milan at 26. Carlo founded seminaries and religious colleges, and worked ceaselessly during the plague of 1576–8, accommodating the sick, burying the dead and risking his own health in doing so. He was canonised posthumously by Pope Paul V in 1610. A huge statue of the saint, familiarly known as San Carlone (big St Charles), stands above Arona. You can climb right up inside the statue and look through his eyes – though it is stifling to do so on a hot summer's day.

# 3

# MONTE MOTTARONE AND SANTA CATERINA

*Climb by cable-car to the Monte Mottarone peak, a natural balcony that overlooks the Alps and lakes; then take a ferry to Santa Caterina del Sasso, an enchanting medieval hermitage that clings to a cliff by Lake Maggiore.*

### Access by Car

Mottarone can also be reached by car (take the road to Gignese from central Stresa). The last section of the road is owned by the Borromeo family, and you will have to pay a toll.

You can also get to Santa Caterina by car in about an hour. From Stresa drive to Intra (18km/11 miles), then take the Intra–Laveno car ferry (20 minutes), and then drive from Laveno to Santa Caterina (5km/3 miles). A short walk from the car park are the 268 steps down to the church – it is a steep descent.

### Cycling Down

For an exciting ride down the Mottarone hire a mountain bike from either cable-car station (you can take them up in the cable-car for a supplement; tel: 0331-324 300; www.bicico.it).

**DISTANCE** Walking: 1.5km (1 mile); ferry return trip 9km (5½ miles)

**TIME** A full day

**START/END** Stresa

**POINTS TO NOTE**

Choose a clear day for Monte Mottarone and take something warm to wear on the peak. Check out afternoon ferry times to and from Santa Caterina (there is at least one an hour) and note the time of the last boat back. There are no midday boats from Stresa, and for a leisurely visit you need to get the earliest afternoon ferry and come back on the penultimate or last boat. There is no café or restaurant at Santa Caterina, so have lunch either on Monte Mottarone (there are cafés and restaurants at the top) or in central Stresa, or put together a picnic (try Supermercato GS at Via Roma 11).

Between lakes Maggiore and Orta, Monte Mottarone (1,491m/4,891ft) commands a magnificent panorama of misty lakes, snow-crested peaks and the Po Valley. On one of the rare really clear days the view stretches to seven lakes.

From Piazza Marconi in Stresa it is about a 1.5km (1-mile) walk northwest to the **Monte Mottarone cable-car** ❶ (Mar–Oct 9.30am–5.20pm, every 20 minutes; buy tickets at cable-car or online, www.stresa-mottarone.it; charge).

## MONTE MOTTARONE

The journey up to Monte Mottarone takes 20 minutes, but it is worth getting out at Alpino, the first stop, to see the rock gardens of the **Giardino Botanico Alpinia** (Alpine Botanical Garden; Apr–mid-Oct Tue–Sun 9.30am–6pm; charge, joint ticket with cable-car available), with over 1,000 species of Alpine and medicinal plants and a lovely setting over Lake Maggiore.

Once at the upper cable-car station walk for about 15 minutes to get to the **summit** ❷ for the best views. Here you will find **Casa delle Neve**, see ⑪①.

## SANTA CATERINA DEL SASSO

Return to Piazza Marconi, where ferries for Santa Caterina leave from the main landing stage. It is only a 15-minute trip, then from the landing stage you have to climb up 80 steps.

The Carmelite convent of **Santa Caterina del Sasso** ❸ (tel: 0332-668 344; Mar daily 9am–noon, 2–7pm, Apr–Oct daily 8.30am–noon, 2.30–6pm, Nov–Feb Sat–Sun 8.30am–noon, 2–5pm; free), seemingly suspended over a rocky precipice and overhung by crags, is at its most romantic when viewed from the lake. Set on the only stretch of Lake Maggiore that has no banks, the hermitage guards the deepest parts of the lake. According to legend, it was founded by Alberto Besozzi, a shipwrecked 12th-century moneylender who vowed to become a hermit if he survived. In 1195 his piety was said to have been instrumental in averting a plague, and he was rewarded with the building of a hermitage to the 3rd-century St Catherine of Alexandria. A votive chapel was modelled on the monastery on Mount Sinai, where the saint's body was supposedly borne by angels.

Prior to the dissolution of the monasteries in 1770, the sanctuary was variously Augustinian, Ambrosian and Carmelite. After centuries of decline, culminating in the collapse of the church roof in a landslide in 1910, it was saved by Varese province, which dedicated huge resources to its long-term restoration. Since 1975 the sanctuary has been entrusted to a small group of lay brothers led by a Benedictine monk.

*Gothic Frescoes*

The monastic complex, strung out along the rocky ledge, is distinguished by a Gothic belltower, a Renaissance porch and an airy gallery that overlooks the lake and the Borromean Islands. Gothic frescoes in the **chapter house** feature St Eligius healing a horse and the Carmelites' sacred emblem, a later addition. Under the graceful Gothic **loggia** of the monastery is a *danse macabre*, complete with a Grim Reaper. Other scenes depict the vanity of human aspirations: a merchant engrossed in his accounts and an amorous courtier face their mortality.

The **church**, essentially an amalgamation of all previous sanctuaries built on the site, is preceded by graceful frescoes depicting an intertwined trio of female saints, including St Catherine. Inside the frescoed sanctuary, but no longer visible and little more than a fissure in the rock, is Besozzi's cave.

After your tour of the convent catch the next ferry back to Stresa.

Above from far left:
Santa Caterina del Sasso; fresco inside the convent; Monte Mottarone cable-car.

## Food and Drink 🍴

### ① CASA DELLE NEVE

Loc. Mottarone; tel: 0323-923 516; www.casadelleneve.it; Wed–Mon; €

This family-run hotel restaurant enjoys great views of the Monte Rosa chain. The peak is snow-capped from December to March, and many of the specialities here are geared to warm up winter skiers: fondues, braised beef, ragout of pork, jugged deer and ostrich. Lighter fare for summer lunches or snacks includes simple grilled meat, local salamis, cheeses, salads and sandwiches.

# 4

# VILLA TARANTO AND LAKE MERGOZZO

*A short and scenic ferry trip takes you to Villa Taranto and the most famous gardens of Lake Maggiore. Stroll along Pallanza's fashionable promenade, then discover tiny Lake Mergozzo and its enchanting fishing village.*

## Lunch Options

For a picnic buy provisions from Supermercato GS at Via Roma 11, Stresa. An area near the entrance of Villa Taranto is allocated to picnickers; alternatively, picnic on a beach at Lake Mergozzo. Reserve a table in advance if you are lunching in a restaurant on Lake Mergozzo.

**DISTANCE** Ferry: 6km (3¾ miles), walk: 4km (2½ miles), bus/taxi: 8km (5 miles)

**TIME** A half day or leisurely full day

**START** Stresa

**END** Mergozzo

**POINTS TO NOTE**

Ferries to Villa Taranto (45 minutes) are more direct but less frequent than those to Pallanza (35 minutes and a short walk to the villa), so you could simply take the first boat in the right direction. Allow at least an hour, but preferably two (or more) for Villa Taranto. If you want to hire a bike or take a bus or taxi from Pallanza to Mergozzo, ask for advice at Pallanza's tourist office on the waterfront at Corso Zanitello 6/8 by Villa Giulia (tel: 0323-503 249), or call 0323-404 444 for a taxi. Buses are infrequent, but there is a daily service at around 1pm from Pallanza (Piazza Gramsci) to Mergozzo (the Verbania–Domodossola line). The quickest way back to Stresa from Mergozzo via public transport is a bus to Verbania (a more frequent service than that to Pallanza) and a ferry to Stresa.

From the jetty on Stresa's Piazza Marconi take a morning ferry to Villa Taranto (or to Pallanza, *see box, left*).

Most of the boats call en route at **Baveno**, set in the lee of a pink granite mountain. A small, subdued version of Stresa, the resort prospered from quarried pink granite and has been popular with British visitors since Victorian times.

### VILLA TARANTO

Pallanza has some fine gardens, but none of them match those of **Villa Taranto ❶** (tel: 0323-556 667; www. villataranto.it; Apr–Sept 8.30am–6.30pm, Oct 8.30am–5pm; charge). The landing stage, located right in front of the entrance, was created specifically for the gardens when they opened in 1952.

## Creation of the Garden

In 1931 Neil McEacharn, a retired Scottish soldier and passionate horticulturist, saw an advertisement in *The Times* for the estate known as La Crocetta on a hillside in Pallanza. He bought the property and devoted the rest of his life to planting and landscaping the site. What had formerly been an unruly wooded headland was transformed into one of Europe's leading botanical gardens. McEacharn imported plants from five different continents – most notably from Asia. Among them were exotic plants, such as coffee, tea, cotton, lotus blossom, giant Amazonian water lilies and papyrus.

## A Riot of Colour

The gardens have more than 20,000 plant species, and are equally lovely in spring and autumn. Tulip-lined flower beds contrast with exotic aquatic plants; there is also a wooded ravine and a soothing water garden with fountains and ponds. In April and May, cherry blossom floats over violets, narcissi and crocuses, and camellias, azaleas, irises and rhododendrons also all flourish. Summer is the time to see aquatic plants, oleanders, hydrangeas, roses and citrus fruits; autumn for coppery Japanese maples, flowering shrubs and mellow dahlias.

## Giant Lilies

Don't miss the giant water lilies in the Victoria Amazonica Greenhouse. They measure up to 2m (6½ft), with leaves that look like huge green trays. The flowers, which are nocturnal and pollinated by beetles, only live for around 24 hours, and gradually change colour from creamy white to pink and purplish red. The water lily was discovered in 1838 in British Guyana by Sir Robert Schomburgh. The plant was successfully germinated in the Royal Botanic Gardens at Kew, London, and presented to Queen Victoria. Originally named *Victoria regia* in her honour, the lily is now known as the *Victoria amazonica*.

Since McEacharn left the villa to the state, Villa Taranto has been a venue for political summits (held in the villa itself, which is closed to the public), each marked by a tree-planting ceremony. Trees have been planted here by Margaret Thatcher, Helmut Kohl and Giulio Andreotti.

**Above from far left:** mausoleum at Villa Taranto; dahlia in the gardens; giant lilies.

**Tulip Week**
From 25 April to May every year there are 80,000 bulbs in flower at Villa Taranto. The star is the tulip – over 65 varieties are planted. During the week one ticket out of every five sold at Villa Taranto has a stamp on the back entitling the visitor to a free plant or flower cultivated in the garden. Below are stained-glass tulips at the villa.

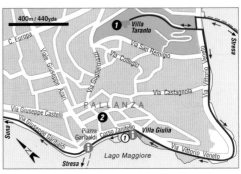

## PALLANZA

Leave the gardens and follow the Via Vittorio Veneto, the lakeside road, for approximately 30 minutes on foot around the headland to Corso Zanitello in **Pallanza ❷**, where magnolia and oleander trees line the quaysides and colourful cafés flank the piazzas.

During the medieval era Pallanza was protected by a castle and was the only town on the lake not to fall under Borromean sway. The resort's mild winter climate, fine views and luxuriant gardens attract the elderly during off-season, while a smattering of bars and clubs in medieval Pallanza draw younger visitors in summer.

Just before the tourist office at nos 6–8 stands the **Villa Giulia**, a frothy pink concoction built in 1847 and originally owned by Bernardino Branca, inventor of Fernet Branca, and now serving as a convention venue. The gardens are a public park and command views of the private islet of San Giovanni, which the conductor Toscanini acquired from the Borromean family.

The enticing **Albergo Milano** – which is actually a restaurant and not an *albergo* (hotel) – overlooks the picturesque old harbour, see ⑪①.

### Suna

The garden-lined lakeside promenade continues for another 2km (1¼ miles). At the far side of the resort you can watch the watersports around **Suna**. This former fishing village buzzes with beach life, although the occasional villa and Romanesque church hark back to a quieter era. If you are contemplating a meal now or later for dinner, the **Boccon di Vino**, see ⑪②, is a homely inn by the landing stage at Suna.

**Right:** Villa Giulia.

*Fondotoce Nature Reserve*

Towards the end of Via Troubetskoy, the promenade merges into the busy coastal road. The 360ha (890-acre) **Riserva Naturale Fondotoce** (www.parchilagomaggiore.it; free) protects the wetlands to the west, habitat of numerous species of waterfowl and other marsh birds. The reserve can be explored by foot or bike along signposted walkways, but the area around Fondotoce is somewhat spoilt by campsites.

## LAKE MERGOZZO

By bus or taxi *(see box, p.38)* it is about 8km (5 miles) northwest from Pallanza to the village of **Mergozzo ❸**. Framed by forests, tiny **Lago di Mergozzo** is one of the cleanest lakes in Europe (motorboats are banned) and the beaches are secluded. Prior to the 9th century it was part of Lake Maggiore, but silt from the River Toce separated it from the larger lake.

Once you arrive at the village of Mergozzo, **Café Portici**, on the main piazza, is the place from which to see the picturesque hamlet as it curves around the fishing harbour; from here inviting alleys and flights of steps lead to a cloistered church and old-fashioned inns.

For a meal you might opt for pasta with scampi or river shrimps at **La Terrazza**, see ⑪③, at the Hotel Due Palme (tel: 0323-80112), which overlooks Lake Mergozzo. Alternatively, sample the tasting menu at **La Quartina**, see ⑪④, or try the gastronomic

delights of **Il Piccolo Lago** ⑪⑤. End with a dip in the clear waters of the lake from its grassy beach.

From Mergozzo catch a bus to Intra/Verbania. Then take the ferry to Stresa.

Above from far left: colourful Pallanza; rooftops of Mergozzo and street scene.

## Food and Drink

### ① ALBERGO MILANO
Corso Zanitello 2/4, Pallanza; tel: 0323-556 816; Wed–Mon, closed Mon dinner; €€€
Frighteningly pricey, but it is worth splashing out for the romantic lakeside location, the exquisite fish dishes and the succulent meat from Piedmont. Needless to say, the food is freshly sourced, the setting elegant and the service faultless.

### ② BOCCON DI VINO
Via Paolo Troubetzkoy 86, Suna; tel: 0323-504 039; closed Wed–Thur lunch in winter; €–€€
The food here more than compensates for the basic decor in this rustic little *osteria*. The blackboard menu offers hearty dishes, like home-made pasta and leeks and casseroles, as well as lighter dishes of fish sourced from the lake.

### ③ LA TERRAZZA
Via Pallanza 1, Mergozzo; tel: 0323-80112; www.hoteldue palme.it; €€
Choose fresh fish or pizza, and enjoy the views of Lake Mergozzo from the terrace of the Hotel Due Palme.

### ④ LA QUARTINA
Via Pallanza 22, Lago di Mergozzo; tel: 0323-80118; www.laquartina.com; €€
Hugging the shore of Lake Mergozzo, this hotel restaurant serves trout and perch from the lake, salami, cheese and game from the hills, and a traditional Piedmontese tasting menu. A delightfully relaxing place.

### ⑤ IL PICCOLO LAGO
Via Filippo Turati 87, Verbania Fondotoce, Lago di Mergozzo; tel: 0323-586 792; Wed–Sun, closed Jan, one week in Nov and Oct–Mar Sun evening; €€€
On the lakeshore road, this is a top-class two-Michelin-starred restaurant with fabulous lake views. Sourcing the finest local ingredients, chef Marco Sacco produces dishes such as smoked Mergozzo trout and Bettelmatt cheese flan with pear mustard and spiced blueberry sauce. Brother Carlo oversees the dining room and wine cellar. A lovely unpretentious interior complements the views.

# 5

# LAKE MAGGIORE EXPRESS

*A combination of lake cruise and mountain railway, crossing from Italy into Switzerland, this tour offers some of the most sensational scenery in Northern Europe. A relaxing three-hour ferry trip is followed by a dramatic railway ride through the wild Ticino mountains.*

**Going Electric**

The 52km (32½-mile) railway line from Locarno to Domodossola opened in 1923. Until recently passengers travelled in vintage carriages with wooden interiors – more romantic but less comfortable than today's electric trains.

**Below:** scenes from Cannobio.

**DISTANCE** Ferry: 61km (38 miles), train: 96km (60 miles)

**TIME** A full day, and the option of extending to a further day

**START** Stresa ferry landing stage

**END** Stresa railway station

**POINTS TO NOTE**

Tickets include both lake cruise and rail journey. Book in advance, especially during high season. Prices are adult €30, child €15 (two days: adult €36, child €18). Contact Navigazione Lago Maggiore: tel: 800-551 801 (from within Italy; free), or 0322-233 200; www.lagomaggioreexpress. com. Services operate Easter–May Thur, Fri, Sat, Sun and hols, June–3rd week Sept Thur–Tue. Passports are essential.

At the Stresa ticket office on Piazza Marconi pick up a ferry timetable and the Lago Maggiore Express leaflet with times of trains from Locarno to Domodossola, and connecting trains from Domodossola back to Stresa.

A two-day ticket allows more time to explore the upper lake and mountain villages, and also includes a free lake pass, allowing unlimited ferry travel.

Begin your tour from any ferry stop on Lake Maggiore. Take the three-hour cruise north to fashionable Locarno in Switzerland, then pick up the panoramic narrow-gauge railway, which travels through the Centovalli (a hundred valleys) and the Valle Vigezzo, down to the town of Domodossola. Views all the way are truly spectacular, from the jewel-like islands of Lake Maggiore to majestic Swiss peaks and scenic valleys. A fast train back to Stresa neatly completes the trip.

## STRESA TO THE UPPER LAKE

From Stresa, the triple-decker *battello* skirts the **Borromean Islands** *(see p.28)* and then stops at the resort of **Baveno ❶** *(see p.38)*. The next stop is **Pallanza ❷** *(see p.40)*, where grandiose villas and a garden-lined promenade overlook the lake. From neighbouring Intra, the boat crosses to Laveno on the eastern side of the lake.

## UPPER LAKE MAGGIORE

The main resorts of the northern lake all lie on the sunny western shores.

Cannero Riviera ❸ occupies a charming site amid subtropical flora, looking over to picturesque islets with ruins of the Malpaga castles *(see margin, right)*. Lovely little **Cannobio** ❹, the last town before the Swiss border, has steep medieval streets located behind a long promenade of pastel-washed façades. If you are on a two-day ticket, this is definitely a place to explore.

## NORTH INTO SWITZERLAND

Across the Swiss border, the first stop is Brissago, which is noticeably more modern than the nearby Italian villages. The larger of the two **Isole Brissago** ❺ (Brissago Islands) is home to the **Parco Botanico del Cantone Ticino**, a botanical garden full of exotic flora, created in 1883 by Baroness Antoinette de Saint-

Léger. She set up residence here and inspired artists, writers and musicians to visit the island.

### Ascona

The boat heads on to **Ascona** ❻, where multicoloured houses line the waterfront. This appealing little resort has always been associated with the arts. Paul Klee, Hermann Hesse and Isadora Duncan were among those who were lured by its charms.

### Food and Drink 🍴
With advance notice you can be served lunch on board the ferry. This is a simple but very adequate three-course meal comprising pasta, fish or meat and dessert with wine included – all for €15. Alternatively, you can buy a picnic from delicatessens in Stresa and have it on board the boat.

**Above from far left:**
Centovalli train climbing a viaduct; view of Cannero Riviera.

**Malpaga Castles**
Dating from the 12th century, the castles belonged to the five Mazzarditi brothers, notorious brigands who plundered local villages. The Visconti destroyed their strongholds in 1414, then a century later the Borromeo family built fortifications here – the remains of which you see today.

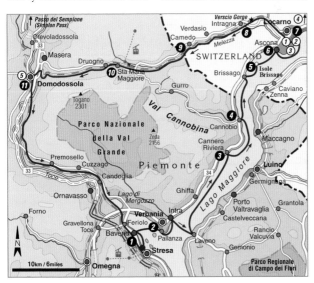

**Lauding the Lake**
Henri-Marie Beyle (better known by his penname, Stendhal) was one of many literati who sung the praises of Lake Maggiore. In a letter to his younger sister in 1811 he wrote, 'When a man has a heart and a shirt he should sell the shirt in order to see Lake Maggiore.'

## LOCARNO

Over the river from Ascona lies **Locarno** ❼, a southwest-facing town with a mild climate and flourishing parks and gardens. Pick up a map when you disembark, or turn left for the tourist office, and locate the nearby station where you will take the train to Domodossola. On a day trip you are likely to have between 1½–3½ hours

in Locarno, depending on which train you opt for.

The heart of Locarno is the porticoed **Piazza Grande**, just back from the lakefront, where you can sit at cafés and watch the fashionable crowds go by. In summer this is the venue for open-air concerts, and in August it hosts the International Film Festival. From the piazza follow the lanes running west of the square for the **Città Vecchia** (Old Town) and Via Cittadella, where **La Cittadella**, see ⑪①, serves excellent pizzas and fish.

*Refreshment*

You may arrive in Locarno too late to lunch in some of the restaurants, but there are plenty of cafés and pizzerias open all day. The most inviting spots are Piazza Grande or lakeside Viale Verbano, where **Al Pozz**, see ⑪②, is open all day for full meals, while neighbouring **Centenario**, see ⑪③, closes at 2.30pm.

*Sanctuary of Madonna del Sasso*

For stunning views of the lake and Alps, take the **funicular** (200m/yds northwest of the landing stage; daily 6.30am–9pm; charge) that climbs up the hill every 15 or 30 minutes (frequency depends on the season), or walk up the pathway flanked by chapels to the **Santuario della Madonna del Sasso** (daily 6.30am–7pm; free), a Capuchin monastery founded in 1480. Here, the **Ristorante/Bar Funicolare**, see ⑪④, is a wonderful spot to admire the view.

## Food and Drink 🍴

**① LA CITTADELLA**

Via Cittadella 18, Locarno; tel: 00 41-0-91 751 5885; Tue–Sun; €€
Downstairs is an informal pizzeria, while upstairs is a smart seafood restaurant; the food at both is delicious. Booking advised.

**② AL POZZ**

Viale Verbano 21, Locarno; tel: 00 41-0-91 744 6364; €€
Open all day every day for pizzas and Mediterranean cuisine, Al Pozz has great views of Lake Maggiore and the mountains from its terrace. *Pollo al cestello* (chicken in a basket) is a speciality.

**③ OSTERIA DEL CENTENARIO**

Viale Verbano 17, Locarno; tel: 00 41-0-91 743 8222; Tue–Sat; €€€
One of Locarno's best restaurants, with traditional Ticino architecture. Fresh local ingredients are used to create dishes like lobster salad, foie gras and stuffed lamb with asparagus.

**④ RISTORANTE/BAR FUNICOLARE**

Via Santuario 4, Orselina, Locarno; tel: 00 41-0-91 743 1833; Feb–Oct; €–€€
Perched above Locarno, at the top of the Sanctuary of Madonna del Sasso, this is worth a trip for the views alone. The short menu is likely to feature *filetto di luccio* (pike), as well as meat and pasta. Alternatively, just go for coffee and cake. Free funicular transport from 5.30pm is offered to those dining at the restaurant.

**⑤ LA PIAZZETTA**

Corso Paolo Ferraris 53, Domodossola; tel: 0324-481 006; closed Mon evening and Sun lunch; €–€€
Welcoming bar/eatery by the station, where you can enjoy a cocktail, snack, pizza or full meal while waiting for your train. The restaurant serves fresh seafood and traditional local dishes.

## CENTOVALLI AND VALLE VIGEZZO

The Centovalli trains depart from below Locarno's **railway station** (Via della Stazione), which is 200m/yds north of the landing stage. Follow directions for Funivia Locarno–Domodossola, and when you board the train secure a seat on the near side for the best views. Once you have emerged from the tunnel, you will be travelling through a wild, spectacular region; the little blue-and-cream train snakes its way slowly around steep, wooded valleys, passing waterfalls and crossing precarious-looking bridges and viaducts high above dramatic gorges. Deepest of all is the gorge of Verscio, a haven for bungee-jumpers.

*Mountain Hamlets*

The railway follows the course of the River Melezza, stopping at neat mountain hamlets, with their chalet-style houses and lofty steeples. **Intragna 8** has a lovely 16th-century bridge, as well as a viaduct (another spot for bungee-jumping). After a customs-check at **Camedo 9** on the border, you are back in Italy. From here, the train climbs up to **Santa Maria Maggiore 10**, which, at 830m (2,723ft), is the highest point of the journey. The village is home to a several art galleries and a little museum dedicated to chimney-sweeping.

## DOMODOSSOLA TO STRESA

The trip ends at **Domodossola 11**, not far from the Simplon Pass. From here you should transfer to the normal Trenitalia rail service for Stresa. (You will need to enquire about platforms.) If you have time to spare and are in need of refreshment, head for **La Piazzetta**, see 🍴⑤, in front of the international station. The final lap of the journey takes just half an hour.

Above from far left: Sanctuary of Madonna del Sasso above Locarno; interior detail; colourful façades on Piazza Grande.

Mountain Hamlets
If you are on the two-day trip, you could alight at one of the villages that give access to a cable-car. From Intragna you can take a cable-car up to Costa and Pila; from Verdasio you can travel to the tiny village of Rasa (the train stops are listed beside the railway seats). All promise spectacular views.

Below left: Intragna.

## Crossing the Border

A fifth of Lake Maggiore lies in Switzerland, in the Italian-speaking canton of Ticino. The resorts are Italian in feel, with their bright piazzas and alfresco eateries, but there is a marked Swiss efficiency about them: while the Italian lakeside villages retain their ancient patina, façades in Switzerland look as though they were painted yesterday. You may be tempted by the stylish shops in Locarno; if so, remember that the local currency is Swiss francs, and although euros are accepted here, you will usually receive change in Swiss francs – often at a poor exchange rate.

# LAKE ORTA

*For all its popularity with Italians and foreigners alike, Lake Orta has managed to retain a certain mystique. This driving tour will transport you to a dreamy pocket of Piedmont, the highlights of which are the medieval village of Orta San Giulio and the magical Isola San Giulio in the centre of the lake.*

**Price of the Peak**
Between lakes Maggiore and Orta, the Mottarone peak commands a wonderful panorama of the lakes and Alps. A road leads up there from Gignese, but be warned: you will have to pay several euros to get there, as the last section is a toll road owned by the omnipotent Borromeo family. You can also access the peak by cable-car from Stresa *(see p.36)*, or on foot.

---

**DISTANCE** 85km (53 miles), returning via Gravellona Toce
**TIME** A full day
**START/END** Stresa
**POINTS TO NOTE**
Avoid Orta on Sundays, when coachloads of visitors descend on the village. If you do not have a car, consider booking an organised tour from Stresa through the Orta tourist office (tel: 0322-905 614). If you are thinking of a meal at Villa Crespi *(see p.48)*, reservations are essential.

---

Separated from Lake Maggiore by the Mottarone peak, Orta is the westernmost of the lakes. Just 14km (9 miles) long and 3km (2 miles) wide, it is tiny in comparison to lakes Maggiore, Como or Garda. It is not so much the scenery that makes it unmissable, but the village of Orta San Giulio and the Isola San Giulio. This little island in the centre of the lake seems to float on the morning mist, and lit up at night it is every bit as magical.

## GIGNESE

Leaving Stresa by car, follow the signs for Gignese and climb the Mottarone.

After 8km (5 miles) you will reach the hill village of **Gignese ❶**, best-known for the **Museo dell'Ombrello e del Parasole** (Umbrella and Parasol Museum; tel: 0323-89622; daily 9.30am–5.30pm; charge), a remarkably large collection of fanciful umbrellas, dating back to 1850. A section upstairs is devoted to the life of local umbrella-makers; the descendants of some continue to make and repair umbrellas. Continue to Armeno and descend southwest towards Lake Orta and Orta San Giulio.

## SACRO MONTE

Take the main approach road passes the entrance to the **Sacro Monte ❷** (Holy Mount; www.sacromonteorta.it). Leave your car in the higher of the two car parks, which is conveniently situated for access to the pedestrianised historic centre of Orta San Giulio.

Sacri Monti are a prominent feature of this corner of the lakes, and Orta's is the finest, rivalled only by the one in Varese *(see p.51)*. Linked to tiny chapels, the Sacri Monti are the climax of Franciscan devotional routes that evoke the symbolic journey through the Holy Land. Set on a wooded hillside, Orta's route wends through a

**Below:** Franciscan statue at Sacro Monte.

series of 20 frescoed chapels, with some 400 life-size terracotta statues that trace the history of St Francis. Slate-roofed Renaissance and Baroque chapels are full of devotional paintings and statues by Lombard artists. The route is well worth following for its peaceful atmosphere and misty views, and the prospect of a light lunch in the **Ristorante Sacro Monte**, see ①①, just within the sanctuary.

## ORTA SAN GIULIO

Set snugly on a peninsula, **Orta San Giulio ❸** has long been a fashionable if discreet resort, known for its chic hotels as much as for its soft light and air of spirituality. Take the atmospheric Via Gemelli from the Sacro Monte to the village. You will emerge outside the Baroque **Chiesa dell'Assunta** (Church of the Assumption), host of a spring concert festival complete with full historical pageantry. The church commands a dramatic view of the sloping **Salita della Motta**, which winds down to the main square, passing geranium-bedecked balconies and Renaissance palaces with peach-coloured façades.

### *Piazza Motta*

The descent ends at **Piazza Motta** by the quaint waterfront. The piazza is lined with outdoor cafés and old-fashioned hotels, including the **Leon d'Oro**, which has a good restaurant, see ①② *(see p.48)*. The hub of village life, Piazza Motta is particularly animated during the Wednesday market. Competition is provided by a handful of delicatessens that sell local produce, such as honey, salami, mushrooms and cheese.

Overlooking the square is the arcaded former town hall, the **Palazzo della Comunità**, frescoes of which

**Above from far left:**
Isola di San Giulio;
quiet backstreet in
Orta San Giulio.

---

## Food and Drink 🍴

**① SACRO MONTE**
Via Sacro Monte 5, Orta San Giulio;
tel: 0332-90220; closed Tue except
in Aug, and Mon pm from Nov–
Easter; €€
An old-fashioned, family-run inn
set in the sanctuary of Sacro Monte;
the lofty lakeside views are complemented by rustic dishes.

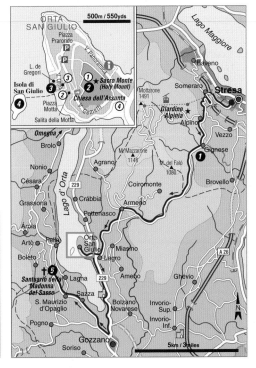

**Parking in Orta San Giulio**

The village of Orta San Giulio is closed to traffic, and cars must be left in the paying parking lots above the centre. From here, in season, you can take an electric tourist train to the centre.

feature a serpent symbol relating to Orta's mythical origins. This façade is an exception in the town – buildings here tend to be painted in muted shades of ochre, green or pink; white is forbidden.

Take **Via Olina**, the main thoroughfare, if you want to indulge in some idle window-shopping in the medieval quarter and perhaps book a table at the charming **Antico Agnello**, see ⑪③.

Not far away, on Largo de Gregori, you will find **Rovera**, a whimsical salami shop that features somewhat tasteless paintings of piglets tucking into a pork feast.

The majority of visitors feel themselves drawn back to the waterfront, where, bathed in soft light, the Isola di San Giulio beckons.

## Food and Drink

**② LEON D'ORO**

Piazza Motta 41, Orta San Giulio; tel: 0322-911 991; €€
An idyllic location, with a long shady terrace overlooking Isola San Giulio, is complemented by a good-value menu of local dishes, including fresh lake fish and wonderful puddings.

**③ ANTICO AGNELLO**

Via Olina 18, Orta San Giulio; tel: 0322-90259; Wed–Mon, daily in Aug; €€
Gentrified rustic taverna in the heart of town offering fresh local produce with a creative twist: home-made pasta, salami, game and risotto dishes.

**④ VILLA CRESPI**

Via G. Fava 8/10, Orta San Giulio; tel: 0322-911 902;
www.hotelvillacrespi.it; Tue–Sun, dinner only Tue; €€€
An imaginative blend of Alpine and Mediterranean flavours, presented in the sumptuous surroundings of a Moorish-style villa. Feast on Sicilian scampi in Martini sauce, ravioli with clams and caviar, crustacean casserole (scampi, prawns and lobster), sea bass with chestnut cream and black truffle – washed down with one of over 1,000 Italian and French wines. Two Michelin stars.

## ISOLA DI SAN GIULIO

At the picturesque jetty, friendly boatmen guide ferries and motorboats to the **Isola di San Giulio** ❹, a tiny car-free island and haven of tranquillity and supplication. In the convent (closed to the public) at the heart of the isle, blue-robed Benedictine nuns devote themselves to contemplation, work and prayer.

Chattering visitors clambering out of boats beside the **Basilica di San Giulio** (daily 9.30am–noon, 2–5.30pm; free) are soon hushed by the sombre mood of this Romanesque church. The island was supposedly overrun by serpents and dragons until AD390, when Julius, a Christian preacher, succeeded in banishing them, before erecting a basilica in celebration. Fragments of the 5th-century church are visible in the crypt.

The church walls are decorated with frescoes, some dating back to the 14th century. The black pulpit, made of local serpentine marble, is a masterpiece of medieval sculpture. Inspired by saintly lore, the work depicts a seething mass of monsters, from grotesque griffins to dragons devouring one another's tails.

### Spiritual Injunctions

The circular **Via Giulino**, which hugs the high walls of the nunnery, carries injunctions to follow the right path. In a bid to evoke 'the island within', there are two pilgrimage paths: the Way of Meditation and the Way of Silence. The island forsakes its silence only in June, when a festival of ancient music is staged.

## SANCTUARY OF MADONNA DEL SASSO

After Orta San Giulio, the other towns on the lake come as something of an anticlimax. Nevertheless, if you have time, it is worth taking the short drive to the sanctuary that overlooks the lake.

From Orta San Giulio, head south along the shore towards Gozzano and follow the western shore to San Maurizio d'Opaglio, an area known as 'tap country' due to the presence of Italy's finest tap- and bath-makers. While these manufacturers prospered on orders from Arab sheikhs, Lake Orta suffered pollution from industrial waste. However, during the early 1990s a cleaning programme coincided with a collapse of the gold-tap market, resulting in waters fit for swimming once more.

Resist the Tap Museum in San Maurizio d'Opaglio in favour of the **Santuario della Madonna del Sasso** ❺, which is just 2km (1¼ miles) away, above Pella. Clearly signposted, it is at the heart of a pleasant series of hamlets. The Baroque frescoed church, built on a granite outcrop over the lake, has fine views over mountains and lake.

### RETURN TO STRESA

You can return to Lake Maggiore by continuing along the western shore, passing Pella, Nonio and Omegna, then heading north to Gravellona Toce and returning to Stresa via Baveno. Or return the way you came, through Gignese, dining perhaps at Orta San Giulio before heading back to Stresa.

### Villa Crespi

If you have a taste for the exotic this is where you will find the magical hotel and restaurant, **Villa Crespi**, see ⑪④, a fairytale Moorish fantasy erected in 1879 by a local cotton merchant inspired by his travels to Baghdad and Persia *(see also p.113)*. The villa is situated out of the medieval centre, at the entrance to the town, so parking is easy.

If by any chance you find that your senses are befuddled by the end of the evening, you might draw comfort from the following philosophical injunction found on Isola San Giulio: 'When you are aware, the journey is over.'

Below: Villa Crespi.

## Alessi HQ

Dedicated shoppers might wish to make a short detour to Omegna, situated just to the north of Lake Orta. The small industrial town has a metalworking tradition that dates back to the 18th century, when pewter was widely produced in the region. Pewter has since given way to the brass, silver, aluminium and stainless steel, but household goods continue to be manufactured here.

One such manufacturer is Alessi (www.alessi.co.uk), internationally renowned for its stylishly designed kitchenware, which ranges from elegant streamlined coffee pots to corkscrews cast in the female form. Alessi's HQ and factory outlet are at Via Privata Alessi 6 in the Crusinallo suburbs. The Forum (Parco Maulino 1; tel: 0323-866 141; www.forumomegna.org; Tue–Fri 9am–12.30pm, 2.30–6pm, Sun 2.30–6pm) is a regional design showcase located in a former steel factory.

# 7

# VARESE AND LAKE LUGANO

*A full-day country and lakeside drive from Varese, nudging the Swiss border on Lake Lugano. A tour of Villa Panza's contemporary art collection is followed by a visit to Varese's nature reserve, then lunch in Luino on Lake Maggiore and a scenic drive along the shores of Lake Lugano.*

**Lake Varese**
Shaped like a battered boot, Lago di Varese is a small lake lying west of Varese. It is a gentle, unremarkable lake framed by rolling hills. From Biandronno on the western shore, you can cross to a tiny wooded island, Isolino Virginia, which has a restaurant and the remains of prehistoric pile-dwellings.

**DISTANCE** 85km (53 miles)
**TIME** A full day
**START/END** Varese
**POINTS TO NOTE**

Check whether the Campo dei Fiori nature reserve (tel: 0332-435 386) is open before you set out. Note also that unless it is a Sunday, holiday or the month of August, you will need to make an appointment to visit Villa Cicogna-Mozzoni (tel: 0332-471 134). Consider making this day trip on a Wednesday, when Luino holds its market (until 4.30pm); the biggest in the region, it sells food, clothes, leather, textiles, household goods, etc. It is a good idea to bring your passport in case you find yourself seduced by the temptation to visit Switzerland.

## Food and Drink 🍴

① **ALBERGO SACRO MONTE**
Via Salvatore Bianchi 5, Sacro Monte, Varese; tel: 0332-228 194; €€
At the top of the Sacro Monte, this small inn has superb views of Lake Varese and Campo dei Fiori nature reserve, as well as first-class food.

## VARESE

Begin in the city of **Varese**. It has long been overshadowed by the popularity of Stresa and Como, but the cleaning of Lake Varese *(see margin, left)*, coupled with effective promotion of the city's villas and gardens, is starting to attract discerning visitors. Essentially a modern industrial city, Varese has styled itself as a *Città Giardino*, or Garden City. It also has a small historic centre, as well as sophisticated shopping.

### Villa Panza

Varese's top cultural attraction is Villa Panza, which houses a major collection of modern American art. From the centre of Varese head north along Via Veratti, which becomes Viale Arguggiari. **Villa Panza ❶** (tel: 0332-283 960; www.fondoambiente.it; Feb–mid-Dec Tue–Sun 10am–6pm; charge) is signposted to the right after about 1km (²⁄₃ mile) from the city centre. Giuseppe Panza, the owner of this frescoed 18th-century mansion, was particularly keen on American abstract artwork, and his collection, with pieces from the 1950s onwards, is strong in work from the 1980s and 1990s.

A clear audio-guided tour leads visitors through the collection's highlights, including abstracts by Phil Sims and David Simpson, and light installations by Dan Flavin.

*Classical versus Contemporary*

Rather than disperse his eclectic collection among his five sons, Panza left it to the Fondo per l'Ambiente Italiano (FAI), the Italian equivalent of the National Trust. As both a listed monument and an art gallery, the villa appeals to both lovers of contemporary art and fans of classical architecture. The former will appreciate the abstract tonal canvases, rooms bathed in brash neon light, bizarre installations and ceilings exposed to the elements. Classicists will admire the old Tuscan chests, Empire-style dining room and magnificent ballroom hung with chandeliers and subdued abstracts.

Beautifully set on the crest of a hill, the landscaped gardens provide a soothing break from the bold artworks.

## SACRO MONTE DI VARESE

If the weather allows, consider making a short visit to the Sacro Monte di Varese (Holy Mount of Varese) and the Parco Regionale di Campo dei Fiori. From Villa Panza return to Viale Arguggiari and head north along the same road for about 6km (3¾ miles), following the signs to Sacro Monte and Campo dei Fiori. A winding road climbs through the heart of Varese's villa zone, where the hills are dotted with *belle époque* and Art Nouveau concoctions perched on grassy knolls.

The **Sacro Monte di Varese ❷** is a major pilgrimage site on the wooded slopes of Monte Campo dei Fiori. Along the steep Via Sacra are 14 devotional shrines with life-size terracotta figures and frescoes. From the **Santuario di Santa Maria del Monte**, and its village at the top, there are vertiginous views down over Lake Varese.

If you are in need of refreshment, stop for a drink or lunch on the panoramic terrace of the **Albergo Sacro Monte**, see ⑪①, on the site of the monastery.

**Above from far left:**
Lake Varese; one of the 14 shrines of the Sacro Monte; Varese, 'City of Gardens'; alfresco drinks in town.

**Below:** detail of art and furniture at Villa Panza.

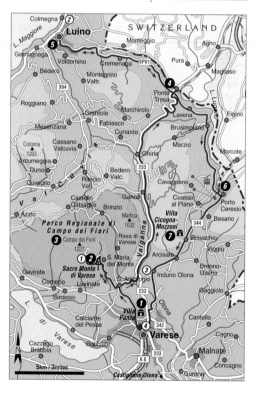

## Lake Lugano

The name Porto Ceresio comes from the Latin name for Lake Lugano – Ceresio – which is still used by Italians. The many-fingered lake lies deep in the mountains between lakes Como and Maggiore. Just over a third of the shoreline belongs to Italy, the rest to the Italian-speaking Swiss canton of Ticino. Steep wooded mountains rising sheer from the water preclude development along most of the shoreline, and Lugano is the only large town.

*Campo dei Fiori Regional Park*

Continue another 5km (3 miles) to the **Parco Regionale di Campo dei Fiori** ❸. Almost at the top of the Campo dei Fiori mountain (1,226m/4,022ft) sits an astronomical observatory; it was conceived by Salvatore Furia, who defused and detonated thousands of unexploded mines to build the road to the reserve. His ambition was to instil in young people his own passion for all aspects of the natural world, from the plants in the ground to the stars in the sky. To this end, the botanical gardens here are an introduction to the surrounding landscape, with woods and valleys framed by the Alps. The observatory specialises in photographing comets through the lens of a powerful telescope. The Campo dei Fiori park comprises six nature reserves and 16 marked trails.

### Food and Drink

**② CAMIN HOTEL COLMEGNA**
Via A. Palazzi 1, Colmegna (2km/1¼ miles north of Luino); tel: 0332-510 855; www.camin-hotels.com; Feb–Nov Tue–Sun, off-season closed for lunch except Wed and Sun; €€
The hotel's two delightful terraces overlook Lake Maggiore, which provides the ingredients for dishes such as carp in sweet and sour sauce and perch fillets with tagliatelle. The villa was built in the early 18th century as part of a hunting estate, and retains a large park with romantic trails and a waterfall.

**③ VILLA CASTIGLIONI**
Via Castiglioni 1, Induno Olona; tel: 0332-200 201; www.hotelvillacastiglioni.it; €€–€€€
This restaurant, set within a beautiful early-19th-century villa, serves traditional regional fare.

**④ HOTEL BOLOGNA**
Via Broggi 7, Varese, tel: 0332-232 100; Sun–Fri; €–€€
This deservedly popular hotel restaurant, located in Varese's historic centre, offers hearty helpings of hams and salamis, fresh pastas, steaks, fish and creamy desserts. Booking essential.

## LAKE LUGANO

From the park retrace your route, pass the Sacro Monte, and take the first road on the left to join the SS233 to **Ponte Tresa** ❹ on Lake Lugano (27km/16¼ miles). The lake, which zigzags across the Swiss border, is wilder and less majestic than Lake Maggiore. Flat waters lap against daunting banks, and the waterfront, with a steep shoreline, is often inaccessible *(see margin, left)*.

Ponte Tresa is a steamer stop and border village, packed at rush hour with Italian commuters travelling to and from Lugano. More peaceful and picturesque is the village of **Lavena**, set on a headland a couple of kilometres (1¼ miles) to the southeast.

### Lunch in Luino

From Ponte Tresa, head west on the SP61 to **Luino** ❺ on Lake Maggiore. You could stop here for a lakeside stroll and lunch, or take the lakeshore road 2km (1¼ miles) north to Colmegna for lunch at the delightful **Camin Hotel Colmegna**, see ②. Encircled by woods, Luino was once a centre for smugglers, whose contraband coffee and cigarettes would pass between Switzerland and Italy as market forces dictated.

### Porto Ceresio

After lunch head back to Ponte Tresa and follow the shore of Lake Lugano as far as **Porto Ceresio** ❻ (10km/6¼ miles), one of the most scenic drives in the province of Varese. A pretty Italian outpost, Porto Ceresio centres on an elegant harbour framed by steep shores.

If time permits, consider a ferry crossing from the Italian port to its Swiss rival across the water. The picturesque village of **Morcote** is set on the tip of the peninsula that runs down the lake towards Italy. Known as the 'pearl of Lake Lugano', it has a maze of alleys and is dominated by a medieval church.

## VILLA CICOGNA-MOZZONI

From Porto Ceresio, take the SS344 south to Varese, stopping after 5km (3 miles) at Bisuschio to visit **Villa Cicogna-Mozzoni ❼** (tel: 0332-471 134; Apr–Oct Sun and holidays 9.30am–noon, 2.30pm–7pm, other days by appointment; charge), an impressive Renaissance stately home inhabited by the genial Count Cicogna-Mozzoni.

The family fortunes were founded on a happy accident: in 1476 Galeazzo Sforza, the powerful duke of Milan, was out hunting when he chanced upon a bear on the rampage. He was saved from certain death by Agostino Mozzoni and his dog. To express his gratitude, the duke of Milan funded a scheme to transform Mozzoni's simple hunting lodge into this lovely villa, complete with Italianate gardens, formal box hedges and fountains.

When the funds are made available, the grand water stairway should be a romantic cascade once more, and the restoration of the frescoes and fountains will be complete. In the meantime, the bohemian, jazz-loving Count Cicogna-Mozzoni continues to host receptions and film shoots as a way to finance the return of his home to its full splendour.

*Dinner Options*

To end the day in style, dine in **Villa Castiglioni**, see ⑪③, a sumptuous 18th-century villa-hotel at Induno Olona, just north of Varese on the road back from Villa Cicogna. Alternatively, if you are heading back to Varese, opt for the good-value restaurant of the **Hotel Bologna**, see ⑪④.

Above from far left: lake view near Ponte Tresa; wild flowers in Campo dei Fiori Regional Park; Porto Ceresio on Lake Lugano.

# Tuscan Gem in Lombardy

Aficionados of art and architecture should not miss the old quarter of Castiglione Olona, 11km (7 miles) south of Varese, off the SP233. If you stumble upon this incongruous little enclave, sitting forlornly among the industries of the Olona Valley, you would be forgiven for thinking it was a Renaissance town in Tuscany. It owes its splendour to Cardinal Branda Castiglioni (1350–1443), who spent time living in Florence and brought the fashionable new style of the Tuscan Renaissance to his native Lombard village. He also brought with him the leading Florentine artist, Masolino, and other Tuscan painters, to decorate the monuments of his citadel. The frescoes that decorate the baptistery and depict the *Life of John the Baptist* are arguably Masolino's finest surviving masterpieces.

# VILLA CARLOTTA
# AND BELLAGIO

*Spend the morning exploring Villa Carlotta's gorgeous gardens at Tremezzo, then catch a ferry to Bellagio, the 'pearl' of Lake Como, where you can wander the town's cobbled alleys, shop for silk and stroll in the grounds of Villa Serbelloni or Villa Melzi.*

**Below:** Villa Carlotta façade and garden.

**DISTANCE** Tremezzo to Bellagio by ferry: 3km/2 miles; walking in Bellagio: 2–4km (1¼–2½ miles), depending on sites covered
**TIME** A full day
**START** Villa Carlotta
**END** Bellagio
**POINTS TO NOTE**
If you are travelling to Villa Carlotta from Como (35km/22miles) allow 40 minutes by hydrofoil or about 90 minutes by ferry. The last boats back to Como from Bellagio leave at around 8pm. Reserve a guided tour of Bellagio's Villa Serbelloni at the tourist office by the pedestrian landing stage of Bellagio (tel: 031-950 204).

## CENTRAL LAKE COMO

The inspiration of writers, artists and composers, Lake Como is the most romantic of the three main Italian lakes. It has long been famed for its natural beauty, fine panoramas and sumptuous villas and gardens. The lake is shaped like an inverted Y, caused by the division of an ancient glacier that carved out its valley. The three branches of the lake converge at the Punta Sparivento (the 'Point that divides the Wind'), the setting of famous Bellagio, 'pearl of the lake'.

Historically adored by the British, Lake Como is now more popular with Americans, due to its superb hotels, clever marketing and the mystique

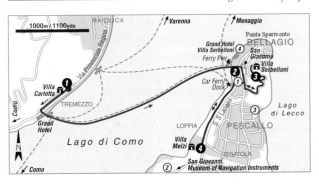

surrounding Bellagio. (As a tribute to this tiny lakeside resort, Las Vegas has its own, splendidly kitsch, Bellagio Hotel.) Picturesque Bellagio is Lake Como's calling card, with Villa Carlotta and its glorious Baroque gardens as the highlight. This central stretch of the lake – embracing Menaggio, Bellagio, Tremezzo and Varenna – is definitely the most seductive.

## VILLA CARLOTTA

**Villa Carlotta ❶** (tel: 0344-40405; www.villacarlotta.it; daily Apr–Sept 9am–6pm, Oct–Mar 9am–4.30pm; charge) has its own landing stage, but you can also access it via Tremezzo (450m/yds to the south) or Cadenabbia (1km/²/₃ mile to the north), which has a car-ferry service.

Graced by magnificent gardens, the villa was a wedding present from a Prussian princess to her daughter, Princess Carlotta of Nassau. Carlotta established a small court here, and completed the landscaping of the gardens in the 1860s. As a result, guests are greeted by a prosperous Baroque pile, bordered by a profusion of pink and white azaleas and a theatrical staircase that leads up to orange and lemon terraces. The focus is on the interplay between villa and lake, as well as the changing perspectives provided by the terraced gardens.

### Inside the Villa

The villa inevitably plays second fiddle to the gardens; its large formal rooms contain a mixed collection of paintings and neoclassical statuary by Canova, including the much-vaunted *Cupid and Psyche*, symbol of the villa, which is a copy of the original in the Louvre.

### Exotic Gardens

The dazzling azaleas and rhododendrons provide a colourful contrast to the villa's cool neoclassical interior. The ornamental pool in front of the villa marks the way from whimsical grottoes to rose arbours, and to the rockery and palm collection on the banks above. Further up are clusters of heathers, magnolia and azaleas, a rhododendron grove and a moody glade of ferns, complete with rushing stream. The plants evoke an exotic map of the world: cedars of Lebanon, Egyptian papyrus, Japanese maples and banana trees, Chinese bamboo, Indian tea, Mediterranean agaves, ferns from New Zealand, eucalyptus and succulents from Australia and giant sequoias from South America.

Allow plenty of time for the gardens. There are 5.6ha (14 acres) and over 500 species of trees and shrubs, including 150 different varieties of azaleas and rhododendrons. April and May are the best months to see the blossom.

### Tremezzo

A short walk south is the resort of **Tremezzo**. While its heyday was in the 1930s, it retains a courtly grace, epitomised by the Grand Hotel Tremezzo. This delightfully mothballed affair remains popular for both wicked weekends and whirlwind gardening-club tours.

**Lake of Seduction**
Henry James was well aware of Lake Como's reputation for illicit trysts: 'It is commonly the spot to which inflamed young gentlemen invite the wives of other gentlemen to fly with them and ignore the restrictions of public opinion.' It was here, according to locals, that President Kennedy romanced Marilyn Monroe.

## Beef up on Bellagio

Bellagio has its own hugely informative website, www.bellagio lakecomo.com. Whether it is wine bars, silk shops, B&Bs, motorboats or guided mountain tours, you will undoubtedly find it here.

## BELLAGIO

From Tremezzo frequent steamers cross the lake to **Bellagio ❷**, situated on the wooded promontory where the two arms of the lake converge. Walks around this cape afford sublime views of mountains in all directions, most notably north to the often snow-capped mountains along the Swiss border.

On Bellagio's bustling waterfront peaches-and-cream houses lead to a promenade lined with oleanders and

## Food and Drink

### ① LA BARCHETTA

Salita Mella 18; tel: 031-951 389; Apr–Oct Thur–Tue; €€
Long-established lake-fish and seafood restaurant, situated up one of the steep, narrow alleys from the waterfront. You won't get the lakeside views, but there is a heated bamboo-covered terrace, service is friendly and the food is a cut above the average eatery on the lake. Meat features on the menu as well as fish.

### ② SILVIO

Via Carcano 12, Loppia; tel: 031-950 322; www.bellagiosilvio.com; €–€€
An unpretentious restaurant that benefits from a tranquil setting above the lake. It serves some of the freshest lake fish in Bellagio, caught by the family who run the restaurant.

### ③ LA PERGOLA

Piazza del Porto 4, Pescallo; tel: 031-950 263; www.lapergola bellagio.it; €
In the tiny fishing port of Pescallo, a 10-minute walk through vineyards from Bellagio, this attractive inn specialises in inexpensive lake fish, which you can eat beneath a pergola. It is worth booking for meals in the evening and on Sunday.

### ④ MISTRAL

Grand Hotel Villa Serbelloni, Via Roma 1; tel: 031-950 216; www.villaserbelloni.com; Apr–Nov Thur–Tue, dinner only during summer; €€€
The Michelin-starred restaurant of this grand hotel produces 'molecular cuisine' (think ice creams cooled by liquid nitrogen) and Mediterranean specialities. Eat in a wood-panelled restaurant, evocative of the great lake steamers, or on the lakeside veranda.

limes. There are red-roofed houses, pastel-tinged façades, steep cobbled alleys, quaint craft shops, a Romanesque belltower and lakeside vistas.

### Shopping along Salita Mella

To explore one of the prettiest alleys, take the steep **Salita Mella**, just opposite the passenger landing stage. There are some lovely shops here, such as Seta di Como at no. 10, selling hand-painted silk handbags and scarves; La Boutique del Borgo (nos 18–22), an outlet for Dolce & Gabbana, Aspesi and Galetti; and artist Pierangelo Masciadri's shop at no. 19, where you can buy beautiful scarves and ties with designs inspired by classical mythology, Renaissance paintings and rationalist architecture. Bill Clinton, George W. Bush and Bill Gates are among those who have commissioned ties from Pierangelo – he has thank-you letters to prove it.

Just before Pierangelo's shop, on the left at no. 18, is **La Barchetta**, see ⑪①, a good choice for regional cuisine if it is time for lunch.

Climb to the top of the street and turn left for **Piazza della Chiesa**, whose church of **San Giacomo** retains its Romanesque belltower. The piazza is the meeting point for tours to Villa Serbelloni.

### Villa Serbelloni

For the best views from Bellagio, join an afternoon tour of the gardens of **Villa Serbelloni ❸** (guided tours only – reserve in advance, *see box, p.54*; weather permitting, tours start from the medieval tower in Piazza della Chiesa;

Apr–Oct Tue–Sun 11am and 3pm; charge). Not to be confused with the exclusive hotel of the same name on the lake, the villa itself belongs to the Rockefeller Foundation and is not open to the public. The steep and winding path takes you high above Bellagio, through fine gardens, for stunning panoramas of both sides of the promontory.

## Villa Melzi

Having explored some of the steep alleys, return to the lake. You can't get lost – all of the alleys lead down to the waterfront. Turn left at the lake for a gentle lakeside promenade to **Villa Melzi ❹** (Lungolario Manzoni; tel: 339-457 3838; www.giardinidivilla melzi.it; Apr–Oct daily 9am–6pm; charge), an austere neoclassical villa set in the first 'English' gardens on the lake.

Although the villa, owned by Duke Gallirate Scotti, is a private residence, the romantic grounds enchant visitors. An atmospheric grotto opens onto Japanese water gardens cleverly concealed from the lake. An intimate mood is created by an ornamental pool,

which is framed by cedars, maples, camphor and myrrh. On the formal terraces above, classical statuary gives way to gently rolling lawns bordered by a pine grove. Below, standing guard by the lake, is a quaint gazebo that captivated Stendhal and Liszt. Beside this bold folly, an avenue of plane trees leads along the shore to the villa, chapel and boatyards, with lofty vistas interspersed with banks of camellias. Compared to Villa Carlotta, which is awash with colour, Villa Melzi favours subtle shades of green and a low-key mood.

## Eating Options

For lunch or dinner, avoid the waterfront tourist traps in favour of the best fish restaurant, **Silvio**, see ⑪②, a short walk from Villa Melzi, or **La Pergola**, see ⑪③, facing the port in Pescallo. If you fancy an extravagant dinner on a luxury hotel's lakeside terrace, before a water-taxi ride home to reality, consider **Mistral** in the Grand Hotel Villa Serbelloni, see ⑪④. Otherwise, wait for a ferry in Bar San Remo on the waterfront.

**Above from far left:** lakeside dining on Como; Bellagio.

**Marine Museum**
In the hamlet of San Giovanni, the new Museum of Navigation Instruments (Piazza Don Miotti; tel: 031-950 309; www.bellagiomuseo.com; summer only 10am–1pm; charge) displays over 200 marine-themed exhibits, including antique sundials, compasses and 18th-century Venetian telescopes. The museum is about half an hour on foot in the Villa Melzi direction; alternatively, take the Trombetta Express – the tourist train that departs from the ferry station and does a circuit of the peninsula.

**Below:** details from Villa Melzi.

# COMO TOWN AND BRUNATE CABLE-CAR

*Explore the historic quarter of Como on foot. Visit the glorious Gothic-Renaissance cathedral, hit the shops for fashion and silk, and take a cable-car ride to the village of Brunate for wonderful views across Lake Como.*

### Sons of Como

Como's most famous sons were Pliny the Elder (AD23–79), the Roman scholar who wrote the 37-volume *Historia Naturalis* (Natural History) and died during the eruption of Vesuvius in AD79, and his nephew and adopted son, Pliny the Younger (AD61–113), an author and lawyer, who is said to have owned at least two villas at Bellagio: one on the hilltop for study and reflection, and another on the lakeshore for hunting and fishing.

**DISTANCE** 6km (3½ miles)

**TIME** A half day

**START/END** Piazza Cavour, Como Town

**POINTS TO NOTE**

For a list of silk and other outlets, ask at the tourist office on Piazza Cavour (unfortunately, they won't divulge any recommendations). If money is no object, make an advance reservation for dinner in the Villa d'Este *(see p.61)*. Alternatively, a far cheaper option, which also requires advanced booking, is a night cruise from Como, with onboard dinner, dancing and live music. Night cruises depart from Como at 9.10pm in summer only (mid-June–Sept), normally on a Saturday. For information see www.navigazionelaghi.it or call 800-551801 (free; within Italy only).

**Below:** the stripes of the Broletto.

## COMO TOWN

The biggest resort on the lake, **Como Town** is a somewhat disconcerting combination of a historic city and a bustling commercial centre. The town has an interesting medieval quarter and some lustrous shops, but there is nothing approaching the intimacy and timelessness of the small villages beside Lake Como. Whether or not Como conforms to your idea of the perfect holiday resort, it is a handy springboard for exploring the lakes region and has a magnificent setting at the end of the western arm of Lake Como.

*Como Town's History*

Since its earliest days, when it rose to prominence as a Roman town, Como has been an industrious, aspirational place. In the 11th century it became a free *comune* (city state), but in 1127 it was destroyed by Milan for having sided with Barbarossa, the German Holy Emperor. From 1335 Como came under the sway of the Milanese ruling dynasties, becoming famous for its silk production.

The Romanesque style, which is particularly pronounced in Como, has been woven into the city's architectural fabric, from churches to fortified medieval towers. Many monuments also owe much to the craftsmanship of the *maestri comacini*, the medieval master-builders and sculptors of Como, who perfected the Lombard style and became renowned throughout Europe for their remarkable skills.

## A TOWN WALK

Begin this walk around town at **Piazza Cavour ❶**, the city's waterfront square and focal point for tourists. Flanked by the terraces of outdoor cafés, it is always bustling with ferry traffic.

*Como's Duomo*

A little way inland along Via Caio Plinio II, **Piazza del Duomo** represents the best introduction to the medieval quarter, centred as it is on the splendidly solemn cathedral. The construction of the **Duomo ❷** (daily 8am–noon, 3–7pm; free) began in 1396, and it has recently been restored. Look out for the cathedral's impressive gabled façade, and observe how it spans the transition in style from late Gothic to Renaissance, with a richly sculpted

main portal. Statues of Pliny the Elder and Pliny the Younger occupy the niches to the left and right respectively.

The interior is slightly gloomy but full of Renaissance works of art, including paintings by Gaudenzio Ferrari (*c.*1471/81–1546) and Bernardino Luini (1480–1532), two Lombard painters who were both influenced by Leonardo da Vinci.

Adjacent to the cathedral is the **Torre del Comune** (belltower), and the magnificent pink-, white- and grey-striped **Broletto**, the former town hall. The latter is an elegantly arcaded Gothic affair, with triple-arched windows.

*Shopping for Silk*

From here, take **Via Vittorio Emanuele II**, which is the main shopping thoroughfare, to **Piazza Medaglie**

**Sant'Abbondio**

In a less salubrious area of Como, south-east of the centre, is the Romanesque gem of Sant'Abbondio (Via Sant'Abbondio; daily 7am–6pm; free). This simple church was the work of the *maestri comacini* (see p.58). The apse is decorated with a remarkable cycle of mid-14th-century frescoes of the life of Christ.

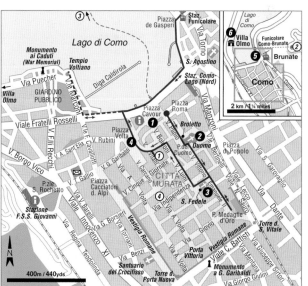

**Above from left:**
San Fedele; detail
from a marble relief
inside the basilica;
lakeside promenade.

d'Oro, stopping at silk shops and fashion emporia. One recommendation is Picci, at no. 54, which supplies silk for Armani. This fine outlet has been here for four generations, and produces crêpe de Chine scarves as well as hand-finished silk ties. Other classic silk shops are on Piazza San Fedele and Piazza Cavour. Bear in mind that the greater the number of colours used within the design, the higher the cost is likely to be.

## Piazza San Fedele

From Piazza Medaglie d'Oro, head back towards the waterfront. If you want to take a break for a coffee at this point, check out **Aida**, a historic café and *pasticceria*. It is located at no. 34 on **Piazza San Fedele**, an attractive medieval square with porticoed houses, which is on the left as you head back along Via Vittorio Emanuele II. Overlooking the square stands the remodelled Romanesque basilica of **San Fedele ❸** (daily 8am–noon, 3.30–7pm; free), which was, in all probability, Como's first cathedral. It is worth walking to the rear of the church to admire the striking apse.

## Silk Skills of the Comaschi

The citizens of Como, known as Comaschi, seem to have couturier skills in their blood: they have manufactured silks, velvets, brocades and damasks since the 16th century. Although silkworms are no longer bred around the lake, Chinese thread is woven and dyed here to the exact specifications of leading Milanese fashion houses. Mantero and Ratti, two of the city's great silk families, supply big-name designers such as Chanel, Dior, Versace and Yves Saint Laurent. While almost all the superstar fashion houses have showrooms in Milan, many either come from the lakes, or – like the Versace dynasty – have villas on Lake Como. The silk and textile industry has made an immeasurable contribution to Como's prosperity and gracious living. On the outskirts of the city is the Museo Didattico della Seta (Museum of Silk; Via Castelnuovo 9; tel: 031-303 180; www.museosetacomo.com; Tue–Fri 9am–noon, 3–6pm; charge). The museum documents the story of Como's silk, with sections on silkworm-breeding and silk-making processes.

## Refreshment

From the square, continue towards the lake along **Via Luini**, crossing Via Cinque Giornate for **Bolla**, at Via Boldoni 6, considered one of the best ice-cream parlours in Como. Take the first left, and left again for **Via Vitani**, which has some of city's finest old mansions. At No. 16, the inviting little **Osteria del Gallo**, see ⑪①, is ideal for a light lunch.

## Piazza Volta

From Via Vitani turn left (east) into Via Muralto and follow the street to **Piazza Volta ❹**. Flanked by boisterous outdoor cafés, the square also has a statue of Count Alessandro Volta (1745–

1827), a self-taught physicist who invented the battery and after whom the volt in named. In summer the square is a venue for concerts, as well as occasional sightings of George Clooney, Como's favourite adopted son.

If you wish to investigate Volta's legacy further, then walk to the western side of the harbour where you will find the neoclassical **Tempio Voltiano** (Volta Temple; Tue–Sun, Apr–Sept 10am–noon, 3–6pm, Oct–Mar 10am–noon, 2–4pm; charge). On display are Volta's personal effects and the batteries that he invented.

## BRUNATE

Return to Piazza Cavour. If the weather is fine, you might wish to take lunch in the elevated environs of **Brunate**, which is set high above the city. Facing the water, turn right and follow the lakeshore north to **Piazza de Gasperi**, passing the city's most upmarket cafés and hotels. The **cable-car 5** to Brunate leaves at half-hour intervals until midnight in summer, and the journey to the summit takes seven minutes.

Once at the top, you can enjoy a rustic lunch at the **Trattoria del Cacciatore**, see ⑪②, 150m/yds from the cable-car station. From Brunate there are outstanding views of the Alps, the lake and an array of 19th-century villas. This is also a good vantage point from which to see the city's octagonal Roman layout. Brunate can also be reached on foot from Como (along the Salita Carescione), and makes a good starting point for hikes into the hills.

*Evening Stroll and Dinner*

In the evening join the throngs on a stroll along the waterfront from Piazza Cavour to the stately **Villa Olmo 6**, which is set in splendid Italianate gardens (winter 9am–7pm, summer 8am–11pm; free). Major art exhibitions are hosted within the villa from mid-March to the third week of July.

For dining, choose between the splendour of the **Villa d'Este**, see ⑪③, in Cernobbio, two ferry stops away, or Como's intimate **Le Soste**, see ⑪④, back from the waterfront.

**Below:** Tempio Voltiano in Como.

## Food and Drink

**① OSTERIA DEL GALLO**
Via Vitani 16, Como; tel: 031-272 591; Mon pm and Tue–Sat; €
Simple, cosy, bistro-like trattoria, with green checked tablecloths and cockerel (*gallo*) ceramics and prints on the walls. Pop in for delicious wafer-thin slices of bresaola from Valchiavenna in Switzerland, plus home-made soups, pasta and cakes, and good cheeses and prosciutto. Lunch or evening snacks (until 8pm) only.

**② TRATTORIA DEL CACCIATORE**
Via Manzoni 22, Brunate; tel: 031-220 012; €€
A traditional trattoria with fine lake and mountain views from its vine-clad terrace. Polenta and *funghi* dominate a short and simple menu.

**③ VILLA D'ESTE**
Via Regina 40, Cernobbio; tel: 031-3481; www.villadeste.it; Tue–Sun; €€€
The setting is a palatial 16th-century villa amid luxuriant gardens at Cernobbio. Formal Italian *haute cuisine* is served on the veranda (jackets and ties are required in the evening), while The Grill, underneath the plane trees in summer, offers regional dishes in a more informal atmosphere. *See also pp.65 and 114.*

**④ LE SOSTE**
Via A. Diaz 54, Como; tel: 031-266 024; Mon–Sat; €€
An elegant bistro that serves dishes such as *radiccio* risotto in red wine and gnocchi with prawns and swordfish. Patronised by discerning businessmen and romantic couples looking for somewhere away from the crowds.

# RAMO DI COMO & VILLA DEL BALBIANELLO

*Begin this tour with a romantic cruise along the beautiful Ramo di Como, past waterfront villas and gardens. After lunch on a haunted island, take a short boat trip to Villa del Balbianello, which has the finest setting on the lake.*

### Catching the Ferry

This cruise starts at Como, but Isola Comacina and Lenno are also accessible from Bellagio, Tremezzo or any of the ferry stops on the Como–Colico service. Note that the yellow-headed columns on the ferry timetable are for Sundays and holidays only. It is easy to make a mistake if you are not used to the system.

**DISTANCE** 60km (37-mile) ferry trip (return)

**TIME** A full day

**START/END** Como Town

**POINTS TO NOTE**

Check ferry times from any landing stage on the lake or on www.naviga zionelaghi.it. If you plan to have lunch at the Locanda dell'Isola Comacina *(see p.65)*, reserve a table in advance and take plenty of cash (it is an expensive restaurant and credit cards are not accepted). Before setting off, study the complex openings and access for Villa del Balbianello. For visits to the villa itself (rather than the gardens), make an appointment in advance. Both the Locanda and the Villa del Balbianello are closed off-season.

## RAMO DI COMO

**Below:** rowing boats beside the lake.

From Como, catch a ferry that stops at Isola Comacina (the faster *aliscafo*, or hydrofoil, bypasses the island). Boats depart from **Piazza Cavour ❶** on the Como waterfront, where you can buy tickets. The cruise leads to the central part of the lake, famed for its villas and gardens. En route it criss-crosses the most beautiful arm of Lake Como, the **Ramo di Como**, moving from the sunny western side to the shady eastern side. The west has the best resorts, historic villas and gardens; the wilder east is dotted with Romanesque churches and the odd silk factory.

*Celebrated Villas*

On the western shore, **Cernobbio ❷** is the first major resort after Como. The town has an appealing lakefront and old quarter, but the most eye-catching sights are the 19th-century **Villa Erba**, which belonged to the family of film director Luchino Visconti before becoming a conference centre, and the Renaissance **Villa d'Este**, the most prestigious hotel in the lakes *(see feature, p.65)*.

After **Torno ❸**, on the eastern side, you can glimpse in the distance the sombre **Villa Pliniana**, where Byron, Stendhal and Liszt stayed, and where Rossini composed the opera *Tancredi* (1813).

Romantic **Moltrasio ❹**, back on the sunny side of the lake, features the deceptively low-key **Villa Versace**, designed as a perfect setting for fashion shows. This was the favourite of Gianni Versace's four homes – and

the one where he chose to be buried. The villa was regularly visited by a string of celebrities *(see feature, below).*

### The Clooney Effect

The Hollywood star George Clooney bought the Villa Oleandra at **Laglio ⑤** in 2002. (The chances are there will be someone on your boat pointing out the beautiful 25-room mansion on the waterfront.) House prices in the vicinity have since soared. Villa Cassinella in nearby Lenno fetched €15 million and Villa delle Magnolie in Moltrasio €12 million – and more celebrities are moving in.

### AMALFI COAST

The **'Amalfi Coast'**, so named because its dramatic cliffs and wild atmosphere are reminiscent of the real Amalfi Coast near Naples, begins just to the north of Torno, on the eastern shore.

The fine Romanesque church in **Pognana Lario** sits in the shade of surrounding villas, while **Nesso**, also on the shaded side, is known for a long Romanesque bridge and a gloomy five-storey silk factory that closed in the 1950s, when silk production moved to China, Brazil and Turkey. From Nesso, the ferry crosses to

*Above from far left:*
*Villa d'Este in*
*Cernobbio; yachts*
*and jetties; Laglio.*

Below: Nesso.

## The A List

Lake Como is a haven for celebrities, who tend to be discreet and whose privacy is respected. Frequent visitors – often guests of the Versace fashion dynasty – include Elton John, Madonna and Bruce Springsteen. George Clooney has a lovely waterfront villa at Laglio; Sting and Ryanair owner Michael O'Leary have homes on the lake; and Richard Branson is the latest celebrity to have ensconced himself in a lakeside villa – at Lenno. Villa del Balbianello has featured in a variety of movies, such as *A Month on the Lake* (1995), starring Vanessa Redgrave and Uma Thurman, *Star Wars Episode II: Attack of the Clones* (2002) and the James Bond movie *Casino Royale* (2006).

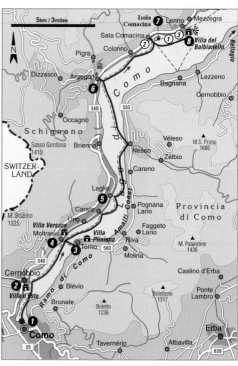

Argegno **❻**, with its red-tile roofs and sunny lakefront. Perch abound in this, the lake's deepest section.

## ISOLA COMACINA

Tiny **Isola Comacina ❼** is the only island in Lake Como. Alight here if you are planning to eat at the **Locanda dell' Isola Comacina**, see ⊕①. It gets very busy at weekends, so aim to be there at 1pm for lunch, or 8pm for dinner.

The island becomes a focus of attention during the **Festival of San Giovanni** (St John), the most magical festival in the lakes, celebrated on 24 June *(see p.20)*.

On the far shore of the lake is the blighted fishing village of **Lezzeno**, in contrast to splendid **Bellagio**, which commands the point beyond *(see p.56)*. Due to the gigantic shadow cast by the mountains, the sun is permanently blotted out, and the locals pay the price in terms of tourism.

### Haunted Island

Tiny though it is, Isola Comacina became a political and military centre in the Middle Ages, acquiring the name of Crispoli, City of Gold. But the island was cursed by the bishop of Como in 1169, probably in revenge for its alliance with Milan, and Como's soldiers razed

**Right:** Isola Comacina, just off shore.

its churches and forced the inhabitants to take refuge in Varenna. The Baroque **Oratorio di San Giovanni** and the ruins of medieval churches are all that remain. More recently, the island was bequeathed to Belgium's King Albert I, who donated it to the state in 1927. Today it is under the supervision of Milan's Brera Academy of Fine Arts.

### Exorcising the Demons

In 1949 a passing English journalist by the name of Frances Dale apparently came up with the idea of a 'rite of fire' exorcism to stimulate the tourist trade – and the word spread like wildfire. Today guests at the Locanda are welcomed by the current melancholic master of ceremonies, the bobble-hatted Benvenuto Puricelli (who was born in Sala Comacina, facing the island, and who served a stint as head chef at London's Penthouse Club). Puricelli has been exorcising the island's demons on a daily basis for the past 30 or so years, in which time the roster of visiting international celebrities has included Sylvester Stallone, Michael Schumacher, Arnold Schwarzenegger, Brad Pitt and Ruud Gullit. The inn's gallery is full of portraits of such stars participating in the theatrical 'purification ceremony'.

### Set Meal and Ceremony

For all the hokum, the set meal – ranging from an array of antipasti to chunks of Parmesan, baked onions, grilled trout, chicken and orange ice cream – is good. The rite of fire begins at the flambéed-coffee stage, and involves arcane incantations and copious amounts of brandy and sugar. Even if the ceremony is not your cup of capuchin, the lakeside views are simply gorgeous. After lunch you may want to follow a path that passes the ruins of the Romanesque churches sacked in 1169.

## Food and Drink

### ① LOCANDA DELL'ISOLA COMACINA

Isola Comacina, tel: 0344-55083/56755; www.comacina.it; closed Nov–Feb and Tue off-season, and occasionally Mon and Wed; €€€
Even if the food was not a draw, people would still flock here to the Locanda for its exclusivity and the bizarre 'rite of fire' *(see left)*. The set menu of regional food has hardly changed since the restaurant opened in 1947. You can reach here via the public ferry or the island boat service from Sala Comacina. No credit cards.

## Villa d'Este

The Villa d'Este was built in 1568, when Cernobbio was a village of fishermen and woodcutters. In 1815 Caroline of Brunswick – princess of Wales and future queen of England – fell in love with Lake Como, and persuaded the owner, Countess Pino, to sell her the villa. Caroline spent five years at the Villa d'Este, following a disastrous marriage to the Prince of Wales (the future King George IV). The couple had found each other equally unattractive (he had married 'the vilest wretch this world was ever cursed with' to pay off his debts), and within a year they were living apart. Caroline spent her time embellishing the villa, and leading a lavish and, by all accounts, lascivious lifestyle. Having run up debts, she returned to London in 1820 in an abortive attempt to take her place on the throne. Legally, Caroline remained Queen Consort until she died at the age of 53. Unlike George IV, she had been popular with the London public, as she had been with the locals of Cernobbio.

Since 1873 the Villa d'Este has been the most luxurious hotel on the lake, hosting royalty, politicans and film stars, and maintaining the elegance of a bygone era.

## Villas and Vistas

In the Renaissance and Baroque eras, patrician villa owners eagerly embellished the natural surroundings. Employing sculptors, painters and landscape gardeners, they created airy loggias as well as Mannerist frescoes, parterres and pergolas. Lakeside vistas were framed by topiary and terraced gardens. The finest example on Lake Como is Villa Balbianello. Other villas of note on the lake are villas Melzi, Serbelloni and Carlotta (see p.55).

Good alternative options for lunch off the island are the **Locanda La Tirlindana**, see ⑴②, by the landing stage where boats cross to Isola Comacina, or **Trattoria Santo Stefano**, see ⑴③, on the main square in Lenno.

## VILLA DEL BALBIANELLO

Set on the tip of a wooded promontory between Lenno and Sala Comacina, **Villa del Balbianello** ❽ (tel: 0344-56110; www.fondoambiente.it; mid-Mar–early Nov Tue and Thur–Sun 10am–6pm; charge) enjoys the loveliest setting on the Italian Lakes. Romance, peace, seclusion, tranquillity and fabulous gardens: this ochre-coloured villa has everything you might hope to find in the region. To access the villa, you can get a boatman at Isola Comacina

to ferry you across, or take the public ferry to nearby Lenno, where you can be taken across in the private shuttle boat (look for the sign at the landing stage). Another option, if it is a Tuesday, Saturday, Sunday or public holiday, is to walk from Lenno to the villa (about 1km/²/₃ mile; signposted from the church square).

### A Cardinal's Retreat

In 1786 the sybaritic Cardinal Durini bought the villa here as a retreat from his taxing diplomatic missions. He incorporated what remained of a medieval Franciscan convent, which, with its quaint pair of belltowers, you can still see today. After landscaping this rocky spur, he enlarged the villa, and, as his crowning achievement, added the loggia on the highest point.

**Right:** sumptuous style at the romantic Villa del Balbianello.

Durini wanted both a memorable venue for literary salons and a place from which to admire the sun setting in the mountains.

The most recent owner of the villa was the wealthy explorer Count Guido Monzino, a descendant of the cardinal. Acquiring the property in 1954, the count restored the villa and filled it with his own collection of books, furniture and works of art. On his death in 1988, he left the villa, complete with contents, to the FAI (the Italian National Trust). Famous for his mountaineering feats and Arctic expeditions – he led a North Pole expedition in 1971 and the first successful Italian ascent of Everest in 1973 – he turned the villa into an international centre for the study of explorations.

Visits of the **villa** take in the library, with hundreds of books devoted to explorations, and a museum full of mountaineering memorabilia, including the sledge on which Monzino trudged to the North Pole in 1971. Fine though the interior is, more impressive is the **loggia** when seen from outside: it is covered in climbing plants, and an old fig tree clings to its columns.

*Romantic Gardens*

The **garden** makes the most of its setting on a rocky spur and the poor soil conditions. Somewhere between a classical 18th-century Italian affair and a romantic English garden, it exploits the gnarled outline of the barren rock to present beguiling paths that lead up to a three-arched folly.

Bound by boxwood and laurel hedges, pergolas, climbing plants and scented wisteria, this secret garden is mirrored in the lake. Cypresses, holm-oaks and plane trees pruned into candelabra shapes provide shelter for snowdrops, cyclamen and magnolia. Closer to the villa are lakeside vistas framed by terracotta tubs of pink hydrangeas and classical statues that protrude from beds of azaleas.

The final view is of the Italian flag unfurled on the jetty, in keeping with Monzino's will. The explorer wanted the gesture to be 'in memory of all the flags my Alpine guides placed on countless peaks all over the world'.

Unless you are up for more adventures, you should ask the boatman to drop you off at the Lenno jetty, where you can take a ferry home.

Above from far left:
Villa del Balbianello.

## Food and Drink

### ② LOCANDA LA TIRLINDANA

Piazza Matteotti, Sala Comacina; tel: 0344-56637; http://tirlindana.lariovalle.com; summer daily, winter Thur–Tue; €€

Facing Isola Comacina, this charming little *locanda* draws food-lovers from afar. Frederic extends a warm welcome, while Patricia produces mouth-watering *ravioli al limone, lavarello con pancetta dorata* (flatfish from the lake in breadcrumbs and bacon), succulent fillet of beef with gorgonzola sauce, and *marquise al cioccolato* to die for. On a warm day arrive early to secure a seat on the terrace, which has glorious views across to the island.

### ③ TRATTORIA SANTO STEFANO

Piazza XI Febbraio 3, Lenno; tel: 0344-55434; mid-Feb–mid-Jan Tue–Sun; www.santostefano.too.it; €–€€

A small sought-after trattoria where chef Claudio Zeni produces delicious lake fish-based dishes at affordable prices. Menus change according to the availability of the freshest ingredients, but are likely to feature fish pâté, smoked trout, ravioli stuffed with mixed lake fish, grilled whole fish, or *missultitt* – small fish that are dried and salted, then fried with vinegar, oil and parsley, and served with slices of polenta.

# BERGAMO

*Bergamo has it all: a majestic setting, a magnificent medieval town, designer shops and gourmet restaurants. This tour takes in one of Italy's richest art museums, then explores the historic Upper Town's piazzas and monuments.*

### Funiculars

Bergamo has two funiculars, both well worth a trip: one connects the Città Bassa to the Città Alta, climbing 100m (330ft) from Viale Vittorio Emanuele II to the Piazza Mercato delle Scarpe – and taking you 500 years back in time (see *p.69*). The other links the Colle Aperto, beyond the Cittadella, to Colle San Vigilio. From here you can climb to the top of Colle San Vigilio for the Castello, a ruined ancient stronghold, and a public park with fabulous views of Bergamo.

**DISTANCE** 4.5km (2¾ miles)
**TIME** A full day
**START** Accademia Carrera
**END** Il Sentierone
**POINTS TO NOTE**

Avoid driving and parking within Bergamo. There are direct train services from Milan or Como, or, if you are killing time before a flight, a half-hourly bus service from the nearby Orio al Serio airport (10–15 minutes). From the train station, catch bus no. 7 to the Accademia Carrara in the Lower Town.

Bergamo has three tourists offices: the IAT by the railway station in Piazzale Marconi in the Lower Town; another IAT in the Upper Town at Via Gombito 13; and the helpful Turismo Bergamo at the airport (daily 8am–11pm). Tickets (lasting 24 hours) are available on the city sightseeing 'hop-on hop-off' bus, which tours the Upper and Lower towns every hour (www.city-sightseeing.it). These tickets are also valid for public transport.

Seen from afar, Bergamo is a mass of belltowers and domes silhouetted against the snow-capped Alps. Originally settled by Celts and Romans, the town nevertheless has a Venetian soul: some 400 years of Venetian rule have left their mark on the town's graceful architecture. There are two distinct centres: the beguiling *Città Alta* (Upper Town) and the more modern *Città Bassa* (Lower Town). The former is bound by a circle of 16th-century walls built by the Venetians after the city expanded beyond its medieval ramparts and fortress.

### LOWER TOWN

This walk begins in the Lower Town, laid out in the 1920s with stately tree-lined avenues, porticoes and piazzas.

### Accademia Carrara and Modern Art Gallery

The **Accademia Carrara** ❶ (Piazza G. Carrara 82/A; tel: 035-399 677; www.accademiacarrara.bergamo.it; Tue–Sun 10am–1pm, 2.30–5.30pm; charge) has a fine collection of Lombard and Venetian art, amassed by a local aristocrat in the 18th century. Among the treasures in this neoclassical palace are Gothic works by Pisanello, and Renaissance and Mannerist works by Bellini,

## Food and Drink

🍴

### ① AGNELLO D'ORO

Via Gombito 22; tel: 035-249 883; Tue–Sun am; €

An atmospheric 17th-century inn in the Upper Town; serves local dishes with polenta or polenta taragna (with butter and cheese).

Veronese, Tiepolo, Tintoretto, Raphael and Mantegna.

Opposite the Carrara is the **GAMEC** ❷ (Galleria d'Arte Moderna e Contemporanea; Via San Tomaso 53; tel: 035-270 272; Tue–Sun Apr–Sept 10am–1pm and 3–6.45pm, Oct–Mar 9.30am–1pm and 2–5.45pm; charge for main exhibitions), hosting temporary exhibitions by sculptors and artists.

## *Shopping*

Apart from art, only shopping is likely to detain you in the Lower Town. The birthplace of the Trussardi fashion dynasty, Bergamo abounds in designer shops. The most elegant shopping district is the arcaded **Il Sentierone**, a pedestrianised promenade lined with cafés and fashion outlets *(see also p.71)*.

## UPPER TOWN

From the Carrara, follow Via della Noca east through the Venetian gateway **Porta Sant'Agostino**, take the Via Porta Dipinta in front of the ex-convent of Sant'Agostino, and climb up into the heart of the **Città Alta**.

**Via Gombito** ❸, a lively medieval street lined by delectable little food shops and eateries, leads into Piazza Vecchia. The **Agnello d'Oro**, see ⑪①, standing back from its little piazza, is a hotel with a characterful restaurant that is famous for its regional dishes.

## *Piazza Vecchia*

A showpiece of both medieval and Renaissance monuments surrounding

Above from far left: the much-touched coat of arms of Bartolomeo Colleoni *(see margin, p.71)*; busy Via Colleoni in the Upper Town; view down to the Lower Town.

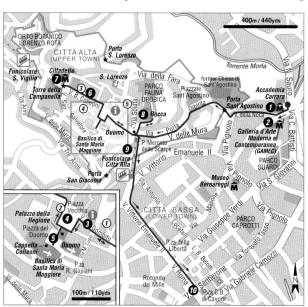

**Above from left:**
Donizetti's piano has pride of place in his museum; Baroque ceiling of the duomo; Colleoni Chapel.

a beautiful fountain with marble lions, the **Piazza Vecchia**  is often described as the most perfect square in Italy.

Flanking the porticoed square is the **Palazzo della Ragione**, the much remodelled medieval council chambers, decorated with a winged Lion of St Mark, the symbol of the Venetian republic. An elegant external stairway leads up to the **main**

hall (open at weekends and for exhibitions only; free), which houses a collection of fresco panels taken from deconsecrated churches and convents in the region.

The new glass lift of the **Campanone** (Belltower; Tue–Fri 9.30am–7pm, Sun 9.30am–9.30pm, off-season weekends only 9.30am–4pm; charge) whisks you up to the top of the tower for fine views. The belltower still chimes some 180 times every evening at 10pm, in memory of the curfew under the Venetians.

Should you be feeling peckish by now, there is nothing more tempting than the terrace of the **Colleoni e dell'Angelo** restaurant, see ⑪②, right on the piazza.

*Basilica of Santa Maria Maggiore*
The religious heart of the town is the adjacent **Piazza del Duomo** ❺, which is home to both the hybrid **Duomo** (Cathedral; currently closed due to restoration) with an 1886 façade, and, submerged beneath a sumptuous Baroque interior, the Romanesque basilica of **Santa Maria Maggiore** (9am–noon, 3–6pm; free). The church has a beautiful Gothic porch adorned with statues and reliefs, and an interior profuse with gilt, stuccowork and paintings. The exquisite inlaid panels on the (roped-off) choir stalls were designed by Lorenzo Lotto, a 16th-century draughtsman from Venice. The charming octagonal **baptistery** on the piazza, to the left as you exit, is a copy of the 14th-century original which used to be inside the church.

## Food and Drink

**② COLLEONI E DELL'ANGELO**
Piazza Vecchia 7; tel: 035-232 596; www.colleoni dellangelo.com; Tue–Sun, closed two weeks Aug; €€€
This 400-year old tavern has a much sought-after terrace on the stunning central square of the Upper Town. Regional and international dishes are beautifully presented in the palazzo's elegant interior. Popular with local businessmen.

**③ DA MIMMO**
Via Colleoni 17; tel: 035-218 535; http://ristorantemimmo.com; Wed–Mon; €€
Two of the seven Mimmi sons carry on the family tradition, producing honest Bergamese cuisine for large numbers of tourists and locals. The setting is a 14th-century palace (stone walls, beams and arches) and a garden which can accommodate 200 diners. Excellent home-made pastas include *casoncelli* (special ravioli with bacon and melted butter) and gnocchi with walnuts and mountain cheese. Follow with T-bone steak, fillet of beef with polenta, fish of the day or sea bass cooked in salt.

**④ VINERIA COZZI**
Via Colleoni 22a; tel: 035-238 836; www.vineriacozzi.it; Oct–Apr Thur–Tue; €
An inviting and innovative wine bar with a huge choice of Italian wines and a varied menu of antipasti, pasta, vegetarian dishes, cold meats and cheeses.

**⑤ OSTERIA DI VIA SOLATA**
Via Solata 8; tel: 035-271 993; www.osteriaviasolata.it; closed Tue and Sun pm, 10 days Feb, 3 weeks Aug; €€€
A tiny, elegant backstreet restaurant where chef Ezio Gritti's exquisite dishes, combining local tradition and haute cuisine, have earned him a Michelin star. Booking advised.

## Colleoni Chapel

Adjoining the church is the ornate **Cappella Colleoni** (Tue–Sun 9am–12.30pm, 2–6.30pm, Nov–Feb until 4.30pm), built in 1472–6 as a mausoleum for Bartolomeo Colleoni, a rich Venetian *condottiere* (mercenary), who demolished the sacristy of Santa Maria Maggiore to create the space.

A masterpiece of the early Lombard Renaissance, this jewel box of a mausoleum has a multicoloured marble façade embellished by medallions, columns, sculpture and reliefs. The interior is no less opulent, with ceiling frescoes by Tiepolo, and the richly carved tomb of the *condottiere*, surmounted by a gold equestrian statue. The tomb on the left is that of his daughter, who died at the age of 15.

## Museums of Archaeology and Natural History

Return to Piazza Vecchia and head west along **Via B. Colleoni ❻**, the continuation of Via Gombito. **Da Mimmo**, see ⑪③, and **Vineria Cozzi**, see ⑪④, are both good options for lunch or dinner.

At Piazza Mascheroni, pass under the Torre della Campanella for the **Cittadella ❼**. This was built in the 14th century as a fortress to defend the west section of the city, then converted by the Venetians as a residence for captains and sailors. Today it is home to the rather dry **Museo Archeologico** and **Museo di Scienze Naturali** (Museum of Archaeology and Museum of Natural History; both Tue–Sun 9am–12.30pm, 2.30–5.30pm; free).

## La Rocca

Retrace your steps back past the cathedral and along Via Gombito to Piazza Mercato delle Scarpe. If you have time, divert left from the piazza along Via alla Rocca and climb up to the 14th-century **Rocca ❽**, which was built on the foundations of the Roman Capitol by the Visconti and reinforced by the Venetians. This is the highest point of the city, with fine views from its park.

Via Solata, located off Via Rocca, is home to the **Osteria di Via Solata**, see ⑪⑤, arguably the best restaurant in Bergamo.

### FUNICULAR TO LOWER TOWN

To return to the lower town, take the 120-year old **funicular ❾** from Piazza Mercato delle Scarpe. The funicular drops to Viale Vittorio Emanuele II. From here walk southeast to the pleasant tree-lined **Il Sentierone ❿**, a favourite rendezvous for the locals and a popular spot for an evening stroll.

### Colleoni's Coglioni

Look closely at the railings of the Colleoni Chapel and you will see the coat of arms of Bartolomeo Colleoni. Called *'i tre colleoni'*, the crest comprises three testicles *(coglioni)* – the third, it seems, endowed by mother nature. Legend has it that touching the coat of arms will bring virility and fertility – hence the gleaming crest on the otherwise black railings!

**Below:** Piazza Vecchia.

### Donizetti

Bergamo-born composer Gaetano Donizetti (1797–1848) is commemorated in the city by a street, a theatre, a memorial, a monument and a museum: the Museo Donizettiano (Via Arena 9; tel: 035-23737; Tue–Sat 9.30am–noon, 2–5pm, Sun 10am–noon, 2–4pm; free) south of the Cittadella. The great master of belcanto opera suffered great tragedy in his personal life. All three of his children died at a young age and his wife succumbed to the plague. Donizetti himself suffered from syphilis, was institutionalised, and died in Bergamo in 1848.

# LAKE ISEO

*Explore the town of Iseo before cruising to the lovely island of Monte Isola for a lakeside stroll and lunch. An afternoon tour of the lake takes in the wild western shore and lakeside villages that retain their medieval core.*

**Spawning Shad**
During the month of June shad come to spawn in the waters of Lake Iseo. You can see caught shad stretched out on wooden frames to dry out; they will eventually be preserved in oil.

**DISTANCE** Driving tour: 72km (45 miles)
**TIME** A full day
**START/END** Iseo
**POINTS TO NOTE**
Check timetables and cruise details at the Iseo tourist office on the waterfront (Lungolago Marconi 2; tel: 030-980 209). The tour of the lake by car is just as lovely by ferry *(see margin, p.74).*

Unfairly neglected in favour of the larger lakes, **Lake Iseo** (Lago d'Iseo) is more tranquil and less self-consciously quaint. The lake is short on the beautiful attractions that are a hallmark of the other lakes, but compensates with fine walks and a gentler way of life.

## ISEO

The best base from which to explore the lake is **Iseo ❶**, a lovely historic town that has not completely sold out to tourism. Until the 1870s it was a significant port that shipped grain from Valle Camonica and steel from the industrial lakeside ports. Today it is a commercial town on a smaller scale. Sandwiched between the waterfront and the feudal Castello Oldofredi, it retains its cosy medieval street pattern and an elegant lakeside promenade.

### Historic Centre

The liveliest part of town is the porticoed **Piazza Garibaldi**, dominated by a statue of the great patriot perched on a mossy rock – this is one of the few horseless statues of the Risorgimento leader. Wind your way to the next flower-bedecked square, **Piazza Mazzini**, where you can see old stone washtubs, then take Via Sombrico and Via delle Pieve for the

church of **Sant'Andrea**. Although clumsily remodelled, it has the finest Romanesque belltower in the region. To the southwest, the restored 15th-century **Castello Oldofredi** is set on a mound and is home to the little **Museo delle due Guerre** (Museum of the Two Wars; Sat–Sun 9am–noon, 3–6pm; free), where two rooms house equipment used in World Wars I and II, including military uniforms, firearms and hand grenades.

## MONTE ISOLA

Return to Piazza Garibaldi and make for the lakeside, where you can take a relaxing ferry ride to **Peschiera Maraglio ❷** on **Monte Isola**, usually the second stop. The mountainous, densely forested island – the largest lake island in Europe – supports a 200-strong community of fishermen, boatbuilders and net-makers.

### Car-Free Island

The pace of life is palpably slow here: private cars are banned, and a minibus service connects the various hamlets. The fishing hamlets reveal refined touches, from sculpted portals to tiny courtyards and loggias. Above, tiers of olive groves merge into vineyards and chestnut groves. The highest peak is surmounted by the 16th-century **Santuario Madonna della Ceriola**, built over a pagan shrine.

### Lunch at Peschiera Maraglio

Choose a typical lakeside haunt at Peschiera Maraglio (which is also known simply as 'Peschiera') for an outdoor lunch. After you have had your fill of grilled sardines, perch risotto and lake scampi, check out the cluttered shop on the waterfront that sells fishing nets and hammocks: net-making is an integral part of life on the island. An industry initiated by Cluniac monks 1,000 years ago now embraces Wimbledon tennis nets and World Cup football nets. Depending on the season and time of day, there may be signs of boatbuilders at work or fishermen laying their catch out to dry in the sun.

### Peschiera to Sensole

The best gentle walk from Peschiera west is along the lakeside path to **Sensole ❸**, taking in views of competent

Above from far left:
Iseo's promenade;
Oldofredi Castle;
view of Monte Isola.

**On Your Bike**
Monte Isola is inundated with visitors in summer and at weekends, but is a delight off-season. You can walk or cycle around the entire island on the lakeshore path (9km/5 miles), or hike up to the island's summit, which commands wonderful lake views. Bikes can be rented from Peschiera Maraglio.

**Below:** Iseo harbour.

## Lake Cruises

The ferry company Navigazione Lago d'Iseo (www.naviga zionelagoiseo.it) not only provides an excellent boat service linking lake villages and islands but offers a variety of reasonably priced cruises during the summer season. On Wednesdays you can take the day-tour cruise, which includes guided visits of historic lakeside villages and Monte Isola. On Sundays (June–7 Sept) there are short trips to all three islands. Saturday nights in season see the romantic Blue Night Cruise, with candlelit dinners and music on board.

swimmers competing for attention with struggling ducks. Both hamlets are set on the sunny side of Monte Isola, and the view encompasses the tiny island of San Paolo with the town of Iseo melting into the background. If you have not already eaten, you might consider **La Spiaggetta**, see ⑪①, between the villages.

## WESTERN SHORE

Catch the ferry back to Iseo, then take a scenic drive clockwise round the lake (following signs west to Sarnico) to see Riva di Solto's rugged western shore in Bergamo province. By contrast, the Brescian bank on the eastern shore is mundane.

### Clusane

Just to the west of Iseo, **Clusane** ❹ *(see also p.79)* is a food-lover's paradise: on the waterfront there are fine fish restaurants that specialise in baked tench, and the Monday market in the main square features stalls laden with cheeses and salami. Crowned by a castle, Clusane overlooks a busy port full of traditional red- and yellow-rimmed fishing boats

setting out in search of tench, pike, chub and lake sardines. The village borders wine-growing Franciacorta *(see p.77)*, and its hinterland is dotted with inns. You may wish to return to Clusane for dinner *(see p.76)*.

### Sarnico to Riva di Solto

The first resort on the western shore (5km/3 miles), **Sarnico** occupies the site of a prehistoric stilt village and owes much of its character to the ruined medieval ramparts and graceful loggias. But it is best-known for its speedboat companies that support one of the lake's premier activities.

Follow the lakeshore road for 20.5km (12¾ miles) to Riva di Solto. From over-quarried Tavernola Bergamasca to Riva di Solto lies the most dramatic stretch of the western shore, with coves carved into limestone cliffs and sheer ravines running down to gnarled rocks. These jagged formations reputedly inspired Leonardo da Vinci's *Virgin of the Rocks* and possibly *The Mona Lisa*. **Riva di Solto** ❺ is a pretty fishing hamlet full of alleys and arches, with placid views across to the domesticated shore of Monte Isola.

**Right:** Pisogne.

## Food and Drink ⑪

### ① LA SPIAGGETTA

Via Sensole 26, Monte Isola;
tel: 030-141 9886; Wed–Mon,
closed evenings; €
This little family-run trattoria serves
simple fish dishes on the lakeside
path between Sensole and
Pescheria Maraglio. Lunch only;
no credit cards; booking advisable.

### Lovere

After 7km (4½ miles) is **Lovere** ❻, dominating the northern end of the lake. Originally a Venetian textile town, Lovere turned to steel then watersports tourism. Stroll along the waterfront with its lakeside cafés and restaurants, then explore the historic core with its narrow alleys, medieval towers, castle remains and the frescoed Renaissance church of **Santa Maria in Valvendra**.

On the lakefront, the neoclassical Palazzo Tadini is home to the **Accademia di Belle Arti** (Via Tadini 40; tel: 035-960 132; www.accademiatadini.it; May–Sept Tue–Sat 3–7pm, Sun 10am–noon, 3–7pm, Apr and Oct Sat–Sun only; charge), displaying works of the Lombard and Venetian schools, including Tintoretto, Jacopo Bellini and Giandomenico Tiepolo.

### EASTERN SHORE

The eastern shore is less peaceful, and between Pisogne and Marone you will be driving through tunnels. Pisogne can be clearly seen across the water from Lovere, but has to be accessed by taking the main Via Nazionale (SS42) north, beyond the northern tip of the lake, and then heading south along the SP55, signposted to Pisogne.

### Pisogne

The former arms-manufacturing town of **Pisogne** ❼ was a centre of commerce for the whole valley in medieval times, and retains an appealing historic centre. The main square is the spacious **Piazza del Mercato**, overlooking the lake and flanked by arcades. Looking onto the square is the medieval **Torre del Vescovo** (Bishop's Tower), where (according to one of the rather finely illustrated information panels in the town centre) those who defaulted on taxes were hung in a cage fixed to the

## The Camonica Valley

North of Lake Iseo, the Camonica Valley (Valle Camonica) has been inhabited since the Neolithic era, when the Camuni tribe first etched itself into immortality. As long ago as 8,000BC hunters were recording scenes of everyday life by carving on the smooth sandstone rocks of the valley floor. Some 180,000 etchings have been discovered, constituting the greatest concentration of prehistoric rock carvings in Europe. These are scattered all along the valley, but the best examples are contained within Capo di Ponte's Parco Nazionale delle Incisioni Rupestri (National Park of Rock Engravings; tel: 0364-42140; Tue–Sun 8.30am–1 hour before sunset, Oct–Feb until 4.30pm; charge), a Unesco World Heritage Site.

Although the Camonica Valley is nowadays partially marred by industry, the park itself is rural and wild, with birch and pine woods. The primitive carvings, known as 'stick men', span several thousand years, from Stone Age scratchings to Bronze Age narratives to Roman graffiti. Animals feature prominently; these range from Etruscan boxer dogs masked as cockerels to elk speared by hunters and deer caught in lassoes. However, unless you are an expert or have booked a guide (tel: 0364-42140 at least two days in advance, around €70 for half a day), the mysteries can be hard to decipher, and the routes are not as clearly marked as you might expect from a World Heritage Site.

tower, and where, in 1518, eight women accused of witchcraft were imprisoned before being burned alive in the square.

### The Poor Man's Sistine Chapel

On the outskirts of the town (follow signs for 'Affreschi del Romanino'), the church of **Santa Maria della Neve** (tel: 0364-87032; Tue–Sun 9.30am– 1.30pm, 3.30–6pm; obtain key from the adjoining Bar Romanino; free) is known as 'La Cappella Sistina dei Poveri' (the Poor Man's Sistine Chapel) on account of the striking frescoes covering the walls and ceiling. Depicting scenes from *The Passion of Christ*, the works are by Romanino (*c.*1484–1559), a leading Brescian Renaissance artist known for his realistic portraits – which can be found all around Lake Iseo.

**Below:** erosion pillar.

### Pyramids of Zone Nature Reserve

Continuing 10km (6¼ miles) south along the lake you come to **Marone**, overlooking the diminutive, privately-owned **Isola di Loreto** (Loreto Island), where trees cluster around a castle.

A twisting road inland from here takes you to **Zone** (7km/4⅓ miles), a picturesque village renowned for the **Riserva Naturale Piramidi di Zone** . This unique formation of 'erosion pillars', created by uneven glacial erosion, is the finest example in Europe. Their most unusual features are the boulders that are precariously perched on top, looking like hats. The best views of these 'stone fairies' (as the locals call them) is at **Cislano**, before you get to Zone.

### Dinner Options

Return to Marone and follow the road south for Iseo (13km/8 miles) to complete the circuit.

For dinner, shoot past Sulzano, unless you intend to take the ferry back to Monte Isola *(see p.73)* for another fish feast (the ferry only takes 15 minutes from here). Clusane is a better bet than Iseo for dining out. Choose from **Punta dell'Est**, see ⑪②, or **Trattoria al Porto** *(see p.79)*, near the waterfront. Alternatively, walk or drive inland from Clusane 1.5km (1 mile) for the enchanting **Relais Mirabella**, see ⑪③, signposted from the main road.

Another lovely setting with first-class food is the **Relais I Due Roccoli**, see ⑪④, at Polaveno, 12km (7½ miles) east of Iseo.

---

## Food and Drink

### ② PUNTA DELL'EST

Via Ponta 163, Clusane; tel: 030-989 060; www.hotelpunta dellest.com; Tue–Sun; €–€€

The fish restaurant of this old-fashioned family-run hotel is *the* place to eat baked tench, the local speciality (baked eel is another). Located on the lake by the ferry landing stage, it also has a car park if you are driving.

### ③ RELAIS MIRABELLA

Via Mirabella 34, Clusane (1.5km/1 mile southwest of the centre); tel: 030-989 8051; Apr–Oct; €€

Above Clusane, with a lovely romantic terrace, this oasis of peace and elegance has wonderful views over the lake. Creative cuisine, including locally sourced fish, is presented with a flourish.

### ④ RELAIS I DUE ROCCOLI

Via Silvio Bonomelli, Colline di Iseo, Polaveno; tel: 030-982 2977; www.idueroccoli.com; €€

This romantic hilltop eyrie above Iseo is a great place for truffles, fresh lake fish, mushroom dishes and chocolate desserts. The dining room has views over the lake, and there is a courtyard for summer dining by candlelight. Also a hotel.

---

# THE FRANCIACORTA WINE TRAIL

*This leisurely drive in the prestigious wine-growing region of Franciacorta takes you through rolling vine-clad hills, past castles, villas and wineries. The trip starts with a visit to a Cluniac monastery and ends with a dinner of baked tench – a local speciality – at Clusane.*

The scenic Franciacorta region south of Iseo is renowned mainly for sparkling champagne-style wines, but also dry, velvety whites and medium-bodied reds. The rolling countryside is dotted with fortified manor houses and elegant villas, many of which have been transformed into flourishing wine estates or inns. Franciacorta owes its prosperity to the work of medieval monks who colonised this hitherto untamed corner of Lombardy.

## Free Court

In the 11th century local nobles called on Cluniac monks to drain the land around Franciacorta. The results were beneficial to both parties: the local economy received a boost, and the way was paved, literally, for the building of impressive new monasteries. The ecclesiastical authorities appreciated the local climate and countryside to the extent that the village of Borgonato became the summer residence of monks from Brescia's Santa Giulia monastery. The secular authorities granted tax concessions, which led to the region's nickname of Corte Franca (Free Court). This in turn encouraged patrician families from Brescia and beyond to build villas in the mellow hills here. Wealthy restaurateurs and viniculturists followed in their wake, and Franciacorta was on the way to becoming the sought-after retreat it is today.

> **DISTANCE** 60km (37 miles)
> **TIME** A half day
> **START** Iseo
> **END** Clusane
> **POINTS TO NOTE**
>
> The majority of the wine estates require prior notice for visits and are only open on specific weekends. The Iseo tourist office (Lungolago Marconi 2; tel: 030-980 209) has all the necessary information and can make reservations for you. Alternatively, contact the Associazione Strada del Vino Franciacorta, the local wine-growers' association (tel: 030-776 0870; www.stradadelfranciacorta.it), which can arrange visits to wineries for individuals or as part of a tour. Castello di Bornato medieval fortress and wine estate is always open on a Sunday, but needs prior notice if you are visiting at other times. For La Montina you must always book in advance.

### Eating Out
Franciacorta is one of Italy's biggest foodie secrets, with many excellent regional restaurants. Places range from roadside cafés with a €10 *menu di lavoro* (workman's lunch) to temples of gastronomy, such as Ristorante Gualtiero Marchesi *(see p.79)*, which are in the arm-and-a-leg bracket.

Above from left:
monastery of San
Pietro in Lamosa;
Bornato Castle;
restored fresco in
San Pietro.

## TORBIERE DEL SEBINO NATURE RESERVE

Coming out of Iseo take a right turn on to the old road to Brescia (avoiding the newer SS510). You will soon see the **Riserva Naturale Torbiere del Sebino** ❶ on your right. This former peat bog is the watery domain of perch, trout and eel. It is also home to a variety of predatory birds, from herons to kingfishers. You can stroll along the paths that go through the peat bogs, perhaps catching glimpses of white swans gliding between the water lilies, or the occasional swoop of a marsh falcon.

## MONASTERY OF SAN PIETRO IN LAMOSA

**Festival Time**
Many wine estates open for tours and tastings during the Festival of Franciacorta on 17, 18 and 19 September – a long weekend of guided tours and gastronomic pleasures.

Towards the southern end of the reserve is the little Cluniac monastery of **San Pietro in Lamosa** ❷ (officially 9am–noon, 3–6pm, but erratic). It sits on a small rise on the right above the road (it is roughly 5km/3 miles from Iseo and easy to miss, so go slowly). Comprising

four chapels, the monastery was founded in the 11th century and added to over the centuries. Sadly it has been neglected, but volunteer restorers in recent years have revealed a number of frescoes – some dating back to Gothic times.

## FRANCIACORTA WINE TRAIL

*Monticelli Brusati*

Head south to Camignone, then follow the marked Franciacorta wine route (marked Strada del Vino Franciacorta) east to **Monticelli Brusati** ❸ and vineyards that stretch out as far as the eye can see. The village is home to **La Montina** winery (Via Baiana 17; tel: 030-653 278; www.lamontina.it; Mon–Sat 9.30–11am, 2.30–4.30pm, Sun 9.30–11am; prior notice required), set around the beautiful Villa Baiana. Monticelli Brusati is also the splendid setting for the **Azienda Agricola Villa** wine estate (follow signs for Villa), complete with farm-stay homes and a rustic inn (tel: 030-652 329; www.villa franciacorta.it) that serves pasta, fresh antipasti and superb wines.

*Bornato Castle*

Retrace your route to Camignone, then drive southwest to **Passirano**, home to a striking medieval castle enclosing modern wine cellars (no access to the public). Turn right (west) for the village of **Bornato**, where the **Castello di Bornato** ❹ (Via Castello 24; www. castellodibornato.com; mid-Mar–mid-Nov Sun and hols 10am–noon, 2.30–6pm; charge) has wonderful views of

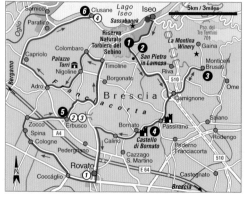

Franciacorta. A crenellated medieval castle, it opens onto a Renaissance villa and Italianate gardens. This is a small wine estate, with tasting included in the visit.

## Erbusco

If lunch is now a consideration, you could stop at the **Trattoria del Gallo**, see ⑪①, at **Rovato**, or head on to **Erbusco** ❺, the unassuming stone-built village at the centre of the wine district. Here you can dine in style at the Michelin-starred **Ristorante Gualtiero Marchesi** at L'Albereta hotel, see ⑪②, or try Tuscan fare at **La Mongolfiera dei Sodi**, see ⑪③.

In any event, Erbusco is worth a stop to visit the **Cantine di Franciacorta** wine shop (on the main road; tel: 030-775 1116). This stocks bottles from all the Franciacorta wine producers: from cheap still wines for a few euros to the superior Ca' del Bosco or Bellavista DOCG sparkling wines. The last both come from prestigious estates nearby, which are only open on specific weekends.

## Corte Franca

After Erbusco, still following the wine route signs, you come to **Corte Franca**, the heart of the wine region, consisting of four villages: Borgonato, Timoline, Colombaro and Nigoline. Among the splendid *palazzi* and villas in this region is Nigoline's 18th-century **Palazzo Torri** (tel: 030-982 6200; Apr–Sept Sun only 3–6pm; charge), furnished with fine period antiques and frescoes.

## DINNER IN CLUSANE

A return to the lakeshore at **Sarnico** marks the end of the wine route. En route to Iseo, you could stop at the fishing village of **Clusane** ❻ *(see also p.74)*. Clusane is known for its baked-tench cuisine – one of the best for tench and other fish is **Trattoria Al Porto**, see ⑪④, in the centre, just back from the lake. If there is time, you might want to take a swim at **Sassabanek** just before Iseo, where there are well-managed pools, a picnic area and a grassy beach on the lake.

**Below:** for a taste of Tuscany.

## Food and Drink

**① TRATTORIA DEL GALLO**
Via Cantine 10, Rovato; tel: 030-724 0150; www.trattoriadel
gallo.it; €€
A retro-looking trattoria, which for years has been dedicated to simple Brescian cuisine. Fish does not get a look in here; typical dishes are steak, rabbit or horse, pastas with *funghi* or truffles, or meat-filled ravioli in a butter and sage sauce.

**② RISTORANTE GUALTIERO MARCHESI**
L'Albereta hotel, Via Vittorio Emanuele 11, Erbusco; tel: 030-776 050; closed Jan–1st week Feb, Sun dinner and Mon; €€€
The region's top gourmet restaurant, where the menu relies on seasonal ingredients. Gualtiero Marchesi was the first Italian chef to be awarded three Michelin stars. All meals are accompanied by great wines, mainly from the finest Franciacorta estates. Booking is essential.

**③ LA MONGOLFIERA DEI SODI**
Via Cavour 7, Erbusco; tel: 030-726 8303; Sept–July Fri–Wed; €€
A rambling former farmhouse that serves fine Lombard cuisine and Tuscan specialities, along with Franciacorta and Tuscan wines. Booking is advised.

**④ TRATTORIA AL PORTO**
Porto dei Pescatori, Clusane; tel: 030-982 9090; Thur–Tue; €
An inviting trattoria by Lake Iseo, renowned for *tinca al forno* (baked tench) with polenta, as well as other freshwater fish. There is a delicious array of desserts too.

# SIRMIONE

*Explore Sirmione, steeped in history and enticingly set on a finger-like peninsula pointing into the southern end of Lake Garda. This walk takes you from the fairytale Scaligeri castle to the evocative ruins of the Grottoes of Catullus, one of the finest Roman patrician residences in northern Italy.*

## Alternative Route

If you prefer to take a more tranquil lakeside route to the Grottoes of Catullus, head north along the Via Panoramica, which skirts the eastern side of the peninsula, and follow the slender pebble beach to the Lido delle Bionde (May–Oct 8am–midnight; free), with pedaloes, a pier and a café. The Grottoes of Catullus are sign-posted from the lido. When the lake water is low you can walk right round the peninsula below the grottoes.

**DISTANCE** 3.5km (2 miles)
**TIME** A half day
**START/END** Drawbridge, Rocca Scaligera
**POINTS TO NOTE**
Sirmione's Old Town is prohibited to traffic except for residents and hotel guests, so park as near as you can to the entrance by the drawbridge. In season and on Fridays (market day) and Sundays this could be in a car park 10–15 minutes' walk away.

Be prepared for narrow alleys packed with tourists, especially from May to September. Pick up a map and other information from the tourist office (tel: 030-916 245) near the entrance of the historic centre at Viale Marconi. If dining at La Rucola, make sure you reserve a table.

## Food and Drink 🍴
### ① LA FIASCA
Via Santa Maria Maggiore 11; tel: 030-990 6111; summer Thur–Tue; €–€€
This central trattoria is a cut above the average tourist Sirmione fare. No-frills classics, regional dishes and home-made pastas are served.

The Romans were drawn to the invigorating waters around Lake Garda *(see p.84)* and, highly impressed by Sirmione's hot, sulphurous springs, developed the spa as a sybaritic retreat. The conquering Scaligeri counts from Verona recognised Sirmione's military potential, and built a medieval fortress from which to govern the southern part of the lake. From the 15th until the end of the 18th century the town was subject to Venetian rule. In spite of recent over-commercialisation, it retains much of its architectural grace.

### ROCCA SCALIGERA

To enter the historic quarter, cross the drawbridge over the moat for the 13th-century **Rocca Scaligera ❶** (Piazza Castello; Tue–Sun, Apr–Sept 8.30am–7pm, Oct–Mar 8.30am–4.30pm; charge). Crowned by swallow-tailed battlements and encircled by water, the fort has guarded the entrance to the historic centre for eight centuries. It was built by the Veronese Scaligeri dynasty, who ruled Verona from 1260–1387. In addition to the picturesque moat, the castle features well-preserved bastions and crenellations, and a fortified dock.

Within the walls is a museum of archaeological finds, but the main attraction is wandering around the battlements and climbing up the towers for views.

From the nightwatchmen's walk the urban views of the densely constructed medieval centre fade into olive groves and the lush Mediterranean end of the peninsula. The area that encompasses the medieval nucleus, the Roman baths and the modern spa starts on the other side of the drawbridge and stretches to the end of the peninsula.

Opposite the castle you will find the tiny 14–15th-century church of **Santa Anna della Rocca** (free). It was also constructed by the Scaligeri family, and for centuries served as a place of pilgrimage.

## VIA VITTORIO EMANUELE

From the castle follow the flow along Via Vittorio Emanuele, the main street leading northwards, and take a right to the pretty 15th-century church of **Santa Maria Maggiore** ❷ (free), which overlooks a narrow beach and lakeside walk. The church has a pretty frescoed portico which incorporates a Roman capital.

On the same street you will find **La Fiasca**, see ⑪①, worth considering for a reasonably priced lunch or dinner. The surrounding web of tiny alleys abounds in cafés, overpriced art galleries, souvenirs and outlets selling chic handcrafted jewellery. This engaging tourist-trap area is relieved by lake views and clumps of palms and parasol pines.

Above from far left: lakeside view of Sirmione; bathing on the rocks; crossing the drawbridge of the Rocca Scaligera.

### Spot the Scaligeri
A recognisable feature of the tyrannical Scaligeri dynasty are castles with fishtail battlements. Sirmione's Rocca Scaligera is a fine example, but there are several others dotted round Lake Garda.

Left: flower-bedecked shop in Sirmione.

### Spa Centre

Via Vittorio Emanuele continues northwards to the modern spa centre of **Terme Catullo** (tel: 800-802 125 within Italy, or 030-916 261; www.termedisirmione.it; Apr–Oct; charge) on Piazza Piatti. Here the hot sulphur springs – bubbling waters are channelled up from the bottom of the lake – are utilised in the treatment of an assortment of respiratory complaints.

### Church of San Pietro

From Piazza Piatti take Via Punta Staffalo which leads to the western shore. Turn right along Via San Pietro, a turning to the north, which brings you to the church of **San Pietro ❸** (closed to the public). This peaceful Romanesque church, the oldest in Sirmione, was constructed on top of the remains of a Roman temple, and remodelled with recycled Roman bricks. Inside are 13th–16th-century frescoes, but the church has been closed to the public since the discovery of ancient tombs.

A lane links the church to the Via Caio Valerio Catullo, leading north to the Grottoes of Catullus.

### GROTTOES OF CATULLUS

Around the end of the promontory, medieval Sirmione can be explored to its Roman core. Crowning the rocky top of the peninsula, and once reached via a triumphal arch and barrel-vaulted arcades, the **Grotte di Catullo ❹** (Via Catullo; tel: 030-916 157; Mar–Oct Tue–Sat 8.30am–7pm, Sun and hols until 5.30pm all year; charge) are the remains of a vast Roman villa and spa complex, constituting one of the most important examples of a Roman patrician residence in northern Italy.

The site was named after Rome's greatest lyric poet, who was said to have languished here when rejected by Lesbia, his mistress in Rome. However, although the pleasure-seeking poet makes reference to a home in Sirmione close to his heart *(see margin, left)*, the general consensus of opinion is that this villa dates from a slightly later period.

## The Ruins

Marking the entrance to the ruins is an **antiquarium** (same hours as Grottoes of Catullus), which displays some beautiful fresco fragments and mosaics discovered at the villa, along with grave finds and sculptural fragments from other parts of Sirmione.

The atmospheric ruins cover some 2ha (5 acres) of the promontory, and are set high above the lake amid olive and cypress trees. A geometric puzzle, the ruins reveal a complex interplay of passages and porticoes – a sensitive blending of brick and rough-hewn stone. The most imposing remains are on the north side, with rooms up to 12m (39ft) long. Deciphering the rooms on the various levels is not easy, but there are plaques on the site showing how the villa was constructed, what the rooms were for and how it would have looked in all its glory. In any event, it is lovely just to wander round the ruins and admire the views.

### EATING OPTIONS

For restaurants, head back towards the castle. If your feet are weary at the end of the day, take the little **Trenino Elettrico** (electric train) which provides a shuttle service (for a small charge) between the Grottoes of Catullus and the Terme Catullo at Piazza Piatti.

For dining, the best (and most expensive) restaurant is the sophisticated **La Rucola**, see ⑪②, close to the castle. Another chic choice is the reopened **Vecchia Lugana**, see ⑪③, but this is out of the historic centre

so you will need to drive or take a taxi. If you are taking a ferry home, you might be tempted to wait for your boat at the **Risorgimento**, see ⑪④, on Piazza Carducci where the ferries depart.

**Above from far left:** Sirmione's historic quarter viewed from the castle; remains of the Grottoes of Catullus.

## Sirmione's Spas

In 1889 a Venetian diver called Procopio inserted a long pipe into the lake rocks near the Grottoes of Catullus, and released a jet of hot sulphurous water. The discovery led to the delicate operation of laying 300m (984ft) of pipes to bring up the steaming waters from the bottom of the lake. Sirmione's first spa centre opened in 1900, and today around 650,000 guests arrive annually for treatment. The waters are rich in sodium chloride, bromine and iodine, and are used for treating respiratory and rheumatic diseases, as well as for beauty and well-being programmes. The Terme *(see left)* combines spa centres and three hotels with thermal facilities. The Aquaria wellness centre at the central Terme Catullo offers five-hour or one-, two- or six-day programmes, where you can make the most of thermal pools, bubbling beds, hydromassage and aromo-chromatic showers. Alternatively, if you want to spare the expense and time, just pop into a pharmacy and purchase a bottle of Acqua di Sirmione or Sirmiogel – both composed of 100 per cent Sirmione spa water.

# LAKE GARDA CRUISE

*Lake Garda's scenery is enormously diverse, from the sea-like southern basin, fringed by beaches, to the fjord-like north, where the Brenta Dolomites drop sheer into the water. This full-day cruise takes in Riviera-like shores, lakeside villages and historic castles and harbours.*

### All Aboard
There are three types of boats: *Battello* ('Batt'), the regular ferry boats, the slightly speedier *Catamarano* ('Cat') and the *Servizio Rapido* ('Sr'), the fastest service, which makes fewer stops and incurs a supplement. There are also *Traghetti*, which are the car ferries that link Toscolano Maderno to Torri del Benaco, and Limone to Malcesine. A *biglietto di libera circolazione* allows unlimited journeys for one day; it is worth buying if you plan to make several stops. There are separate kinds for the whole lake, the lower lake or the upper lake. Services, particularly on the fast boats, are not very regular, so check timings before starting your journey.

**DISTANCE** Hydrofoil from Sirmione to Malcesine: 60km (37 miles); return trip: 120km (75 miles)
**TIME** A full day
**START/END** Sirmione
**POINTS TO NOTE**
Make an early start and take one of the fast routes (marked in red on the timetable – available from the tourist office at the entrance of town) to get to Malcesine for lunch *(see margin, left)*. The boat will make several stops en route (described in this tour). You will only have time to disembark at one destination other than Malcesine. Recommended are either Gargnano or Bardolino. Study the timetable well in advance, and work out the time of your return journey. If you are limited to half a day, concentrate on the lower lake only.
  This trip starts at Sirmione, but you can also go from other resorts on the southern shore, such as Desenzano del Garda or Peschiera del Garda.

Cruising the lake is far more relaxing than coping with traffic-filled lakeshore roads and dimly lit tunnels. It is also the best way to admire the scenery.

Approximately 51km (32 miles) long and 17km (10½ miles) wide at its maximum point, Garda is Italy's largest lake. Apart from some spectacular scenery, it offers fine beaches and clean, warm waters. The area enjoys a wide range of climatic conditions, from chilly Alpine glaciers north of the lake to Mediterranean warmth. The lake acts as a kind of solar battery, and the shores have an abundance of luxuriant vegetation.

In the Middle Ages ruling dynasties built splendid defences around the lake's shores; in the 19th century European aristocrats and literati came for the healthy climate. Although picturesque villages still dot the shorelines and medieval castles rise from the waters, it is nowadays the most crowded of the Italian lakes, with large numbers of German and Austrian holidaymakers, sailors and windsurfers descending on its shores. The south in particular has seen major commercialisation.

### BARDOLINO

From the ferry landing stage off Piazza Carducci in **Sirmione ❶**, take the fast service to **Bardolino ❷** on the Veneto shore, framed by rolling hills and vine-clad slopes. Ideally, wait until the

return trip for a visit here, when you can enjoy the eponymous wine in any of the local bars. Bardolino Superiore now has DOCG status; to learn more about the delicious cherryish-red wine, visit the excellent **Museo del Vino** (Wine Museum; Via Costabella 9, Bardolino; www.zeni.it; mid-Mar–Oct Mon–Fri 9am–1pm, 2–7pm, Sat–Sun until 6pm; free). You can taste whites and rosés as well as the reds, and purchase bottles from two or three euros.

Bardolino is also home to the **Museo dell'Olio di Oliva** (Olive Oil Museum; Via Peschiera 54, Cisano di Bardolino; Mon–Sat 9am–12.30pm, 2.30–7pm, Sun 9am–12.30pm; free), with a shop selling olives, honey and pasta, as well as olive oil. Wine and food aside, the town has a ruined castle, two Romanesque churches and a medieval quarter.

## GARDA

The lake took its name from the town of **Garda** ❸, which shelters in the lee of a huge rocky outcrop. Lake Garda was once called Benacus (Beneficient) – and it is occasionally still referred to by the Latin name. The former fishing village is now a popular resort, with a long café-lined promenade that you can see from the boat, and narrow alleys packed with *trattorie* and souvenirs.

**Above from far left:** shaft of sunlight over the waters of Garda; touring the lake by boat.

**Below left:** barrels of wine in Bardolino.

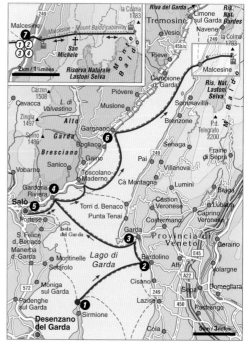

**Freewheeling Down**
For an exhilarating descent down Monte Baldo, hire a mountain bike in Piazza Matteotti in Malcesine, and take it up on the funicular. Paragliders can go up too.

## THE LIMONI RIVIERA

From Garda the boat plies across the lake to **Gardone Riviera ❹** and **Salò ❺**, two prestigious resorts on the Lombardy bank, whose elegant promenades you can admire from the boat. (If you have time on another day, they are covered in more detail in tour 16; *see p.88*).

---

## Food and Drink

### ① OSTERIA ALLA ROSA
Piazzetta Boccara 5, Malcesine; tel: 045-657 0783; www.osteriaallarosa.it; 8.30am–2am summer daily, winter Tue–Sun; €
This authentic family-run *osteria* uses the freshest of local produce and serves traditional regional dishes, such as home-made pasta with chicken liver, polenta with salami, and stewed or fresh grilled fish. Specialities include *olivetto*, an aperitif made with local olives and grappa, and served with canapés, and *sbrisolona*, a delicious cake.

### ② OSTERIA SANTO CIELO
Piazza Turazza 11, Malcesine; tel: 0348-745 1345; www.osteriasantocielo.com; €
An excellent spot for a light lunch, with salads, salamis, tapas and cheese, plus a good choice of wine. The setting is simple and rustic, with a cellar-like interior and tables outside.

### ③ TRATTORIA VECCHIA MALCESINE
Via Pisort 6, Malcesine; tel: 045-740 0469; www.vecchiamalcesine.com; Thur–Tue, dinner only Nov–Mar except Sun and hols; €€€
A tiny gourmet trattoria tucked away on a scenic terrace in the old quarter. The Michelin-starred cuisine includes local delicacies such as duck confit with Parmesan and truffles, ravioli with snails, and prawns with garlic butter. Book in advance.

### ④ RISTORANTE RE LEAR
Piazza Cavour 23, Malcesine; tel: 045-740 0616; www.relear.com; Mar–Sept Wed–Mon; €€€
Ranked as one of the 300 top restaurants in Italy, the King Lear offers innovative combinations such as thin octopus slices in Nori seaweed, rabbit fillet with asparagus polenta, and olive ic cream. Menus change monthly, and vegetarian meals are available on request. The restaurant is in the heart of the Old Town, a stone's throw away from Castello Scaligero, with a terrace on Piazza Cavour.

*Lemon Terraces*

The boat then skirts the loveliest stretch of coast, where wild Alpine terrain stretches all the way to **Riva del Garda**. Despite the towering cliffs, the area is a hothouse for Mediterranean shrubs and citrus fruits as a result of the balmy microclimate.

Citrus fruits, introduced by medieval monks, used to constitute the lake's cash crop. To protect the lemons from rare but catastrophic cold spells, the terraces were traditionally south-facing, covered with wooden supports in the colder months, and watched over by conscientious gardeners who would light fires if the temperature dropped suddenly. Citrus cultivation went into an irreversible decline in the 19th century, with competition from cheaper citrus fruits grown in the hotter climate of southern Italy. These distinctive but mostly defunct *limonaie* (lemon terraces), with their rows of white stone pillars, still dot the lakeshore from Gargnano, north of Gardone, to **Limone sul Garda** *(see box, right)*. The **Castel Lemon Grove** (Mon–Sat 10am–6pm; nominal charge) in Limone is one of the few that has been preserved and can be seen in operation.

*Gargnano*

From Gardone it is a short hop to **Maderno**, twinned with neighbouring **Toscolano**, and used mainly by tourists for its car ferry service across to **Torri del Benaco** on the opposite side of the lake. Going north, **Gargnano ❻** is one of the main sailing centres on the lake, and it is

hard to find a more pleasant lakeside village. Remarkably unspoilt, it has a lively little port, a promenade of orange trees, some charming hotels and two gourmet restaurants. With time in hand, alight here and take a leisurely stroll before boarding the next boat to Malcesine.

## MALCESINE

Alight at **Malcesine** ❼, the loveliest resort on the Veneto shore, with a café-lined waterfront, balconied Venetian-style houses and a maze of cobbled alleys. A quintessential family resort, it is popular with British visitors and buzzes with activity throughout the season. Choose from one of the many restaurants, ranging from simple *osterie*, such as **Alla Rosa**, see ⑪①, and **Santo Cielo**, see ⑪②, to gourmet haunts like **Trattoria Vecchia Malcesine**, see ⑪③, and **Ristorante Re Lear**, see ⑪④.

### Scaligero Castle

The village clusters below the crenellated **Castello Scaligero** (daily May–Sept 9.30am–8pm, Oct–Apr 9.30am–6.30pm; charge), whose battlements and tower command fine views of the lake. Within the walls is a **natural history museum**, which includes the **Sala Goethe**, devoted to the German writer's drawings, notes and views on Lake Garda and the castle. Goethe visited the lake in 1786 when it was under Austrian rule, and while sketching the castle at Malcesine he was arrested on suspi-

cion of being a spy. He was imprisoned here but released soon afterwards, having convinced the authorities of his innocence.

### Monte Baldo Cable-Car

Behind the resort you will find Malcesine's modern **funicular** (tel: 045-740 0206; www.funiviedelbaldo.com; every 30 minutes Apr–mid-Sept 8.15am–6.45pm, Mar and Oct 8.15am–5.45pm; charge), which links the resort to the summit of **Monte Baldo** (2,218m/ 7,275ft). The panoramic rotating cable-cars whisk you up there in a matter of minutes, stopping en route at San Michele. The mountain ridge offers spectacular views, scenic walking trails and a profusion of flora. In winter the cable-car goes up to the ski slopes.

Cruise back to Sirmione, alighting – if you haven't already – at Bardolino en route.

Above from far left: Gargnano, a sailing centre; Monte Baldo cable-car; waterside drinks at Limone sul Garda; rock faces beside the town.

Below: lemons still grow on the terraces at Limone sul Garda; citrus souvenirs.

## Limone sul Garda

Several boats, including a car ferry and private excursion boats, link Malcesine with the busy resort of Limone on the Lombardy shore. Less self-consciously cute than Sirmione, Limone is caught between lush Mediterranean vegetation and sheer rock faces that cower under snow-clad peaks. D.H. Lawrence adored Limone, which, he wrote, overlooked 'a lake as beautiful as the beginning of creation'. What was once an old fishing port is today a tad touristy – for all its bright southern light and pastel façades overhung by flower-bedecked balconies, the service is poor and the souvenirs (mostly lemon-themed) overwhelming. You might assume the village is named after the citrus fruit, but it is more likely that the name derives from the Latin *limen* (border), referring to the former frontier here between Austria and Italy.

# GARDONE RIVIERA

*On the western shore of Lake Garda, Gardone Riviera maintains much of the elegance that drew the rich, royal and famous in the late 19th century. A visit to botanical gardens and Il Vittoriale degli Italiani, the most eccentric residence on the lakes, is followed by a ferry trip to the historic resort of Salò.*

**Below:** details from the Hruska Botanical Garden.

**DISTANCE** Gardone Riviera to Salò by ferry: 4km (2½ miles)
**TIME** A half day
**START** Gardone Riviera
**END** Salò
**POINTS TO NOTE**

If you are not driving, there are regular ferries to Gardone Riviera from Sirmione, Desenzano del Garda or Peschiera del Garda. Villa Fiordaliso restaurant requires advance reservations for lunch or dinner *(see p.90)*. If a trip to Isola del Garda appeals, check out the times of boats from Salò and book a guided tour in advance *(see feature, p.91)*. If the tour is in the morning, start at Salò and visit Gardone Riviera in the afternoon.

It was the mild climate that attracted the Austrian emperor and other members of the European elite to build palatial villas here in the 1880s, as **Gardone Riviera** became the most fashionable resort on the lake. It retains some fine villas, a promenade lined with oleanders, palms and orange trees, and a beach for lake swimming. The guest list at the *belle époque* **Grand Hotel ❶**, which stands prominently on the waterfront, includes Somerset Maugham, Vladimir Nabokov and Winston Churchill (who came to paint the lake and mountains).

## HRUSKA BOTANICAL GARDEN

Just off the lakeside promenade, the **Giardino Botanico Hruska ❷** (mid-Mar–mid-Oct daily 9am–7pm; charge)

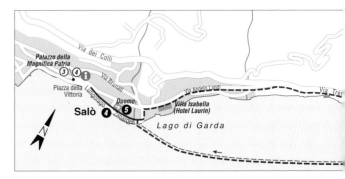

is an oasis of flora created in 1912 by Arturo Hruska, a passionate botanist and dentist to the last czar of Russia. It is a peaceful spot where you can wander among pretty rockeries, an English garden full of tropical plants, a Japanese garden of pools and bamboo, and an Alpine garden with landscaped waterfalls and ravines chiselled out of the rocks.

## IL VITTORIALE

Take a left turn after the botanical gardens and climb up to **Gardone Sopra**, the oldest part of town. This is the site of a much-visited, somewhat bizarre villa, secluded by cypresses and oleanders. **Il Vittoriale degli Italiani** ❸ (tel: 0365-296 511; www.vittoriale. it; Apr–Sept grounds 8.30am–8pm, guided tours of house and war museum 9.30am–7pm, Oct–Mar grounds 9am–5pm, guided tours 9am–1pm, 2–5pm; house closed Mon, war museum closed Wed; charge) is a testament to the megalomania of Gabriele D'Annunzio (1863–1938). A soldier, poet, Fascist, aviator, aesthete and womaniser, he occupies an odd place in Italian hearts,

somewhere between reverence and bafflement. 'Destiny calls me towards Lake Garda,' he declared, although it was actually Mussolini who presented him with the villa in 1925.

### The Dictator and the Poet

Disillusioned with the paltry gains won by Italy in the post-World War I peace – the Dalmatian town of Fiume (Rijeka; now part of Croatia) on the Adriatic had been promised to Italy but was presented to Yugoslavia instead – D'Annunzio and his private army occupied Fiume. Forced to withdraw in 1921, D'Annunzio retired to paint his gilded cage on Lake Garda, while Mussolini pursued his own mythmaking on the world stage. Not that the decadent aesthete and the brutal dictator were by any means soul mates. On one famous occasion D'Annunzio brazenly forced his fellow Fascist to read the following inscription, which he had placed over a mirror: 'Remember that you are made of glass and I of steel'. Mussolini's reaction is not recorded, but D'Annunzio lived to tell the tale.

**Above from far left:**
villa in Gardone Riviera; Hruska Botanical Garden; mausoleum of Gabriele D'Annunzio.

**Nationalist Name**
The fervently nationalist Gabriele D'Annunzio named his eccentric residence 'Il Vittoriale degli Italiani' after the Italian victory over Austria in 1918.

**Below:** Fiat belonging to D'Annunzio.

**Historic Hotel**
One of Salò's loveliest Art Nouveau villas is the Villa Isabella, now the Hotel Laurin (Viale Landi 9; www.laurin salo.com). This was the headquarters of the Italian Foreign Ministry, presided over by Mussolini. It was converted into a hotel in the 1960s.

## Decadent Decor

Named in celebration of Italy's victory over Austria in 1918, and remodelled by D'Annunzio, the 18th-century Il Vittoriale is one of Italy's most flamboyant pre-war estates. The house, known as the **Prioria**, has two reception rooms, one cold and formal for disliked guests (including Mussolini), the other a warmer chamber where his favourites were welcomed. D'Annunzio's delusions of grandeur led him to create a low entrance to his study so guests had to stoop, presumably to bow. The decadent decor raids sacred and profane motifs; walls and ceilings are studded with crests, arcane symbols and secret mottoes. Islamic plates jostle for space with Austrian machine-guns. D'Annunzio abhorred daylight, so the windows were made of stained glass or painted over. When the penumbra became too much to bear, D'Annunzio would retreat to the coffin in the Sala di Lebbroso. His blue bathroom is filled with Moroccan trappings such as trunks of questionable ceramics. In the dining room his embalmed pet tortoise, which died of indigestion, served as a reminder of the wages of gluttony.

The **Museo della Guerra** (War Museum) documents D'Annunzio's military enterprises, displaying uniforms, medals for bravery, banners and numerous photographs.

## Relics of the Fiume Fiasco

The splendour of the **grounds** contrasts with the ugliness of the creations that inhabit them: a magnolia grove houses a war memorial, while the *Puglia* ship that featured in the Fiume fiasco is bizarrely beached among the cypresses. In a hangar are a biplane that flew over Vienna in the war, vehicles that took part in the Fiume debacle, and the Italian flag. The mausoleum, where Fiume casualties are buried, features D'Annunzio's kitsch, self-aggrandising tomb, and, displayed in an eerie museum, his death mask.

Still, pockets of the gardens are less oppressive: a lemon terrace has been transformed into a private garden and the Fascistic amphitheatre has fine views from the top tier.

---

## Food and Drink 🍴

**① AGLI ANGELI**
Piazza Garibaldi 2, Gardone Riviera; tel: 0365-20832; Wed–Mon; €€
A cosy old-world *locanda* near Il Vittoriale, with a terrace for summer dining. Typical dishes are leek flan, risotto, pasta with local Bagoss cheese, duck with pepper and grapes, and lake fish.

**② VILLA FIORDALISO**
Corso Zanardelli 132, Gardone Riviera; tel: 0365-20158; www.villafiordaliso.it; closed Mon and Tue lunch; €€€
This small and stylish Art Nouveau villa-hotel is where Mussolini stayed with his mistress Clara Petacci during the Salò republic. Stroll through the grounds after a gourmet lunch in the seductive Michelin-starred restaurant.

**③ OSTERIA DELL'OROLOGIO**
Via Butturini 26, Salò; tel: 0365-290 158; closed two weeks in Jan and July; €€
A popular inn that serves lake fish as well as more bizarre dishes such as skewered birds.

**④ OSTERIA DI MEZZO**
Via di Mezzo 10, Salò; tel: 0365-290 966; noon–11pm; €€
One of Salò's oldest inns, set in vaulted cellars in the centre. Serves salamis, home-made pasta, *baccala* (dried cod), perch, pike or eel from the lake, rabbit, beef and delicious cheeses.

*Lunch Options*

For lunch the **Agli Angeli**, see ⑪①, is a good family-run restaurant, handy for Il Vittoriale; or, if cash is no consideration and you want the best in town, head for the beautiful Art Nouveau **Villa Fiordaliso**, see ⑪②, right on the lake, with an elegant gourmet restaurant. After lunch, drive or take the ferry to Salò (10 minutes on the fast service, 13 minutes on the normal ferry).

## SALÒ

Set on a beautiful deep bay with a long lakeside promenade, **Salò** is an appealing combination of bustling local town and elegant resort. It was founded in Roman times, then in 1337 became the capital of the Magnifica Patria, a community of 42 towns. During a less fortunate episode of its history, Salò became the seat of Mussolini's puppet republic in 1943 – his last desperate attempt to reorganise Fascism in Italy. A town of fleeting moods rather than awesome sights, it wears its history lightly. After an earthquake in 1901 the resort was rebuilt in airy Art Nouveau style, and is still graced by elegant villa-hotel restaurants.

Stroll along the **Lungolago Zanardelli** ❹ (the lakeside promenade). The waterfront near the centre has some fine arcaded buildings, including the **Palazzo della Magnifica Patria**, the 17th-century town hall.

The most prominent landmark of Salò is the lofty campanile of the late Gothic **Duomo** ❺ (daily 8.30am–noon, 3–6.30pm; free) on the waterfront towards the eastern end of the Lungolago Zanardelli. The church has an elaborate Gothic altarpiece and a number of Renaissance paintings. The piazza in front of the unfinished brick façade and Renaissance portal is the setting for open-air performances of the Gasparo da Salò Festival of music in summer.

For lunch or dinner in Salò there are several lakeside cafés and restaurants, but the better ones tend to be set back from the lake: try the **Osteria dell' Orologio**, see ⑪③, or the **Osteria di Mezzo**, see ⑪④.

### Gasparo da Salò

Gasparo Bertolotti (1542–1609), more familiarly known as Gasparo da Salò, was a skilled craftsman who was one of the earliest makers of violins. He was born in Salò and is celebrated annually with the Gasparo da Salò Festival of Music.

## Isola del Garda

Off the headland south of Salò lies the little cypress-studded Isola del Garda (Garda Island). For centuries this was a monastery island, and the first religious community was said to have been founded on the island by St Francis of Assisi. Since the dissolution of the monastery by Napoleon, the island has been in private hands, and in 2001 was opened to guided tours. The present owners are the Cavazza family. When Count Cavazza died he left the island to Lady Charlotte Chetwynd Talbot and her seven children, the youngest of whom occasionally shows visitors around.

Two-hour tours include the glorious gardens and the neo-Gothic villa, along with tasting of local products such as wine and olives. The island is open to visitor tours from May to September (book in advance, tel: 0365-622 94 or 0328-384 9226). Boats leave from Salò from the ferry ports of Portese or Barbarano di Salò, daily except Wednesday. From June the island can also be visited from Sirmione, Desenzano, Garda and other resorts in the lower lake. For a detailed schedule, visit www.isoladelgarda.com.

# A TASTE OF TRENTINO

*Riva del Garda is Trentino's gateway to Lake Garda, and the castles of Arco, Drena, Toblino and Tenno are all a short drive away. Riva's picturesque location and healthy climate drew the European aristocracy from the early 1800s. Today it is a popular tourist resort.*

**DISTANCE** 60km (37 miles)

**TIME** A leisurely day

**START/END** Riva del Garda

**POINTS TO NOTE**

If lunching at Castel Toblino (Toblino Castle), be sure to make a reservation (see p.95). In summer occasional evening cruises depart from Riva; for information visit www.navigzionelaghi.it or tel: 800-551 801 (within Italy only).

### A Taste of Torbole

The footpath from Riva to Torbole (4km/ 2½ miles) along the waterfront affords fine lake and mountain views. Goethe described Torbole as 'a wonder of nature, an enchanting sight'. The setting is as alluring as ever, but the village is rather spoilt by the main coastal road slicing through. However, this is no deterrent to hikers, free climbers, paragliders, wind-surfers or sailing enthusiasts who descend on Torbole all year round.

## RIVA DEL GARDA

If arriving in Riva by car, park near the castle, ideally in the car park by the waterfront, the Giardini di Porta Orientale, or the adjoining Congress Centre.

As a medieval port for powerful prince-bishops, **Riva del Garda ❶** became a pawn in the dynastic struggles between such city states as Milan, Venice and Verona. In 1703, during the War of the Spanish Succession, the port was sacked by the French, leaving Riva a shadow of its former self. Like the rest of Trentino, Riva was revived under Austrian rule (1815–1918), and it flourished as a fashionable resort, attracting such Mitteleuropean literary heavyweights as Franz Kafka, Thomas Mann and Friedrich Nietzsche. Contemporary Riva draws large numbers of tourists: middle-aged ones off-season, and, in summer, a younger crowd who enjoy the watersports as much as the culture.

### Rocca di Riva

Begin your tour of Riva at the lakeside **Rocca** (Tue–Sun 10am–6pm; charge), the moated medieval castle upon which the resort is centred. This austere military stronghold, which once included an arsenal, barracks and palace, evokes only a partial sense of its former glory.

The Rocca was designed as a fortress, but the Renaissance prince-bishops of Trento turned the interior into a gracious patrician residence. It was further domesticated during Austro-Hungarian times, when its fearsome appearance was compromised by the lowering of its corner towers.

Beyond the drawbridge, the **Museo Civico** (Civic Museum; Piazza Cesare Battisti; tel: 0464–573 869; daily 9.30am–6pm; charge) has a minor art collection, sculpture from regional churches and archaeological finds going back to the Bronze Age. The Rocca is best seen at night when it is illuminated; occasional evening events take place in the castle courtyard.

*Piazza Cavour*

After the Rocca you might hit a lakeside café, or, from the adjoining Piazza Garibaldi, take Via Mazzini to **Piazza Cavour**, the main inland square, which is often obscured by market stalls. Here, you can buy local olives, cheese and wine at the Wednesday market; to sample Riva's best coffee, head for **Caffè Maroni**. The alleys around the square form the heart of the shopping district, and sell clothing and leather goods.

*Piazza 3 Novembre*

Return to the Rocca and head west to the main **Piazza 3 Novembre**, which opens onto the lake. The square is lined with 15th-century Venetian-Lombard palaces, including the town hall. With its 13th-century gateway, a view of the 16th-century bastion above, and **Hotel Sole**, once an Austro-Hungarian rulers' residence, the square is a microcosm of Riva's history. The hotel has lost much of its grandeur, but its sunny terrace is good for drinks and people-watching.

For spectacular views over the lake, take the lift up the **Torre Apponale** (Tue–Sun 10am–6pm; charge). The tower has variously served as a prison, as a store for salt and grain, and as a look-out point during World War I.

## TORBOLE

When you are ready to leave Riva, set off east along the main SS240 for 4km (2¹/₂ miles) to **Torbole ❷**. Presenting the less genteel face of Lake Garda, what was once a fishing village is now a lively watersports centre that benefits from unusual wind conditions. Just

**Below:** mountains and mist.

## Wine Country

Thanks to its microclimate, Garda Trentino is favourable to wine-growing, and vineyards are abundant. The most noteworthy grape is the Nosiola, which produces dry white wines and Vino Santo Trentino. The latter is a sweet dessert wine made with grapes that are dried out on wooden racks and then pressed during Holy Week, before being aged for three years in oak casks.

before midday, the Ora southern wind whips down the lake and fills the sails of windsurfers until early afternoon. On the approach to Torbole you might see free climbers seemingly suspended over the lake in the rocky playground of **Corno di Bo**, just south of the resort.

If lunch is a now priority, you could try the Trentino specialities at Torbole's **Piccolo Mondo**, see ⑪①, by the River Sarca, or, if you fancy lunch in Toblino Castle, start driving north following signs for Arco and Trento.

### ARCO

After 5km (3 miles) you come to **Arco** ❸, a spa once favoured by Austro-Hungarian grand-dukes, and renowned for its gardens and pleasant climate. In the late 1800s the resort was charac-terised by *belle époque* balls, health cures and carriage rides.

#### Arco Castle

The former archducal gardens overlook the wizened stump of the **Castello di Arco** (Apr–Sept 10am–7pm, Oct–Dec, Feb and Mar 10am–4pm, Jan Sat–Sun

only; charge), which looms above the resort and makes a dramatic impact. A steep path winds up to the castle, but the interior, for all its fragments of Gothic frescoes depicting courtly scenes, does little justice to the striking setting.

### DRENA AND TOBLINO CASTLES

Continuing 18km (11 miles) north to Toblino, there are views on the right (beyond Dro) of **Castello di Drena** (Mar–Oct Tue–Sun 10am–6pm, Nov, Dec and Feb Sat–Sun only 10am–6pm, closed Jan; charge). The stark late-12th-century castle, controlling the Sarca and Cavedine valleys, was destroyed in 1703, but has undergone restoration in recent years. Today it serves as a venue for ex-hibitions and conferences. A museum contains local archaeological finds.

**Castel Toblino** ❹ (tel: 0461-864 036; www.casteltoblino.com), set on the tiny lake of the same name, and with an atmospheric restaurant, seems to materialise from nowhere. In his trailblazing *Italian Alps* (1875), the mountaineer Douglas Freshfield wrote of 'the little pool of Lago Toblino, ren-dered picturesque by its castle, an old fortified dwelling defended landwards by crenellated battlements'.

Diners at the **Ristorante Castel Toblino**, see ⑪②, can visit the atmospheric interior, complete with Renaissance courtyard and 17th-century stoves. Others can enjoy an apple strudel and glass of wine in the **bar/café** below (9am–10pm), with a lovely terrace overlooking the lake.

### Adamello-Brenta Park

Retrace your path to Sarche and take the first right turn – towards Comano Terme. The start of this western route skirts the **Parco Adamello-Brenta**, named after the Brenta rock formations, a Dolomite group marked by towering limestone pinnacles and surfaces bathed in a pink-tinged orange sheen. Toblino's vineyards give way to neat barns and lush Alpine pastures, deep forests and sheer rock faces.

## THE ROAD TO RIVA

**Comano Terme ⑤** is a thriving spa resort, valued since antiquity for treatment of skin and respiratory ailments, with its curative waters gushing out of the rocks at 28°C (82°F). Next head for **Bleggio Superiore ⑥** (5.5km/3½ miles), a rambling village in a lovely Alpine setting, well signed from Comano Terme.

From Bleggio follow the signs for **Fiavè ⑦** (5km/3 miles), which has an **archaeological site** (July–Aug 9am–noon, 3–6.30pm) mired in the bogs just outside the village on the Riva road. The nature reserve features the remains of a late Neolithic village.

Continue on the Riva road (the SS421) to **Lago di Tenno ⑧** (11.5km/7 miles), an emerald-tinged lake formed by a landslide. The medieval village of **Tenno ⑨** clustered around a private castle, lies 3km (2 miles) to the south.

From here the road twists down to Riva del Garda. On the approach to Riva, the reappearance of olive groves represents the clearest shift back to the sultry Mediterranean microclimate of Lake Garda.

### Dinner in Riva

For dining options in Riva del Garda, you could choose one of the restaurants overlooking the illuminated Rocca, or the smart **Al Volt**, see ⑪③, north of Piazza 3 Novembre in the historic centre. Alternatively, the **Restel de Fer**, see ⑪④, between Riva and Torbole, is well worth the walk (1.6km/1 mile) or short drive from the centre.

---

## Food and Drink

**① PICCOLO MONDO**
Via Matteotti 7, Torbole; tel: 0464-505 271; www.hotelpiccolo mondotorbole.it; summer daily, winter Wed–Mon; €€
This family-run hotel restaurant serves typically Trentino fare – game, dumplings, mushrooms, polenta and apple strudel – as well as Mediterranean cuisine.

**② RISTORANTE CASTEL TOBLINO**
Sarche; tel: 0461-864 036; Wed–Sun, Mon lunch only; www.casteltoblino.com; €€–€€€
A romantic castle on the enchanting Lake Toblino, offering three set menus (light lunch, fish and meat), as well as à la carte. Snacks are available all day at the lakeside bar.

**③ AL VOLT**
Via Fiume 73, Riva del Garda; tel: 0464-552 570; www.ristorante alvolt.com; mid-Mar–mid-Feb Tue–Sun, dinner only in July; €€
In the elegant little rooms of a historic palazzo you can try Trentino specialities with a modern twist or fish fresh from the lake. There is a large choice of wines: regional, national and foreign.

**④ RESTEL DE FER**
Via Restel de Fer 10, Riva del Garda; tel: 0464-553 481; www.resteldefer.com; €€–€€€
Restel de Fer is a delightful rustic trattoria, which has been run by the Meneghelli family since 1400. Try *zisam* (deep-fried small lakewater fish with onions) or marinaded salmon trout.

# MILAN

*The dynamic business and design capital of Italy presents the perfect urban antidote to the languid atmosphere of the lakes. On this day excursion explore the Duomo, indulge in designer shopping and stroll by night in the arty Brera quarter or lively Navigli.*

**DISTANCE** Minimum 3km (2 miles) on foot
**TIME** A full day
**START** Piazza del Duomo
**END** Brera quarter
**POINTS TO NOTE**

From Como, Stresa, Bergamo or Varese, a direct train journey takes about an hour. From the Stazione Centrale, Milan's main rail station, catch the metro to the Duomo (cathedral). Consider booking a gourmet lunch in Bice *(see p.99)* or perhaps a night at the opera (tel: Infotel Scala 02-7200 3744 or book online at www.teatroallascala.org). A viewing of *The Last Supper* should be booked well in advance *(see left).*

### The Last Supper

Visitor numbers to Leonardo da Vinci's *The Last Supper* (1495–8) shot up after the success of *The Da Vinci Code* – both Dan Brown's best-selling novel and the film adaptation. This means that tickets are not always easy to come by. Book well in advance on 02-8942 1146 (from abroad +39 02-8942 1146; lines open Mon–Fri 9am–6pm, Sat 9am–2pm). The number is often engaged, but just keep on trying! Operators speak English and will give you a code number and time of visit. The refectory where the painting hangs is limited to 25 visitors at a time, and the visits are restricted to 15 minutes.

## Food and Drink 🍴
### ① LE TERRAZZE

La Rinascente Department Store, Via Santa Radegonda 3; tel: 02-877 159; €–€€

On the seventh floor of Milan's most prestigious department store, it is the views of the Duomo roof you come for rather than gourmet food. Find a table outside where you can almost reach across to the pinnacles. As well as lunch and supper, you can come here any time of day for drinks and snacks.

## Fashion and Culture

The lure of Milan for most visitors is the chance to indulge in designer shopping in Italy's fashion citadel. Clothes, accessories, designer objects for the home and luxury foodstuffs represent the best buys. The greatest bargains are to be found in discount stores (often called 'stock-houses'), where last season's stock can be bought cheaply by shoppers prepared to wade through rails of unsuitable goods in un-chic storerooms. Even die-hard anti-consumerists cannot fail to appreciate the sheer extravagance of the visual display in the glitzy designer district.

Further temptation comes in the form of culture on an international scale. If you wish to take in an opera at La Scala, prior booking is essential; otherwise, the Duomo, Milan's cathedral, provides the main cultural treat. The historic city centre is easily manageable for visitors, and the distances between the majestic cathedral and the designer shopping district are walkable.

### THE DUOMO

At its sartorial best, Milan is a cosmopolitan city that puts on a show with panache. Piazza del Duomo is the historical heart of Milan, with the

magnificent cathedral providing the backdrop. The severe square is dominated by the **Duomo** ❶ (www.duomo milano.it; daily 7am–6.30pm, roof 9am–5.20pm, winter until 4.20pm; cathedral free, charge for treasury, baptistery and roof terraces), Europe's largest Gothic cathedral. The capacity is around 40,000 people, and the façade is adorned by 3,000 statues, 135 spires and 96 gargoyles. This unfinished masterpiece was begun in 1386, and seamlessly blends Gothic, Baroque, neoclassical and neo-Gothic styles. French-style flying buttresses and soaring pinnacles contrast with the excessive width preferred by native builders. Make a point of going up to the **terrazzi** (roof terraces), either by lift or (the slightly cheaper option) by

clambering up 158 steps. For access to both, go to the back of the Duomo. Apart from fine views of the city and, on very clear days, as far as the Matterhorn, you can admire the gilded figure of the sacred **Madonnina**, the city's protector, soaring over Gothic spires.

*La Rinascente*

Just off the square, **La Rinascente** (Via Santa Radegonda 3), the city's most upmarket department store, makes a possible first port of call for shopping. Its panoramic rooftop restaurant, **Le Terrazze**, see ⑪①, overlooks the spires of the cathedral. If food shopping is on the agenda, then head for **Peck** (Via Spadari 9), a gastronomic temple west of the cathedral.

**Above:** *The Last Supper* by Leonardo da Vinci.

**Aperitif Hour**
The after-work happy-hour *aperitivo* has become very much a Milanese way of life. Stylish bars and cafés serve a sensational range of cocktails, with *stuzzichini* (snacks) and elegant canapés.

**Below left:** view of the Duomo.

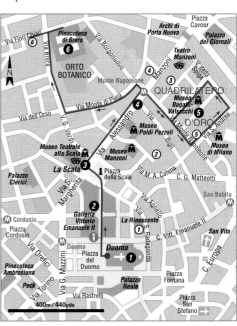

**Above from left:**
Galleria Vittorio
Emanuele II; head to
the Quadrilatro d'Oro
for fashion; Navigli
canal quarter; court-
yard of the Pinaco-
teca di Brera.

**Museo Poldi Pezzoli**
You won't have time
for many museums on
a day trip to Milan but
this one is a real gem
– and not too big.
You will pass it en
route from La Scala to
the fashion shopping
district. The Museo
Poldi Pezzoli (Via
Manzoni 12; www.
museopoldipezzoli.it;
Tue–Sun 10am–6pm;
charge) contains an
exquisite collection
of Renaissance paint-
ings, antiques and
curios which belonged
to Gian Giacomo
Poldi Pezzoli, who
owned the palace
in the 19th century.
On his death he stipu-
lated that the building
and contents should
be accessible to
the public.

**Below:** you can walk
on the roof terraces of
the Duomo.

## GALLERIA VITTORIO EMANUELE II

Connecting Piazza del Duomo with La
Scala opera house is the **Galleria
Vittorio Emanuele II ❷**, a splendidly
arcaded shopping gallery and rendez-
vous known as *il salotto di Milano*
(Milan's front parlour).

Among the restaurant/bars here,
**Savini** (tel: 02-7200 3433) has been
welcoming stars from La Scala since
1867. This is the place for Lombard
classics, but its formality can be oppressive. Among the Galleria's best bars is
the Art Nouveau **Zucca in Galleria** at
no. 78 (the Duomo end). It is a classic
spot for an *aperitivo* – especially a Campari, as Davide Campari, the inventor
of the drink, was born here on the first
floor. Other perfect people-watching
spots include café/restaurant **Biffi** (tel:
02-805 7961) and, next door, the **Gucci
café**, which serves good snacks.

## LA SCALA

The Galleria leads to Piazza della Scala,
home to **La Scala ❸** *(see also p.96)*,
Italy's most celebrated opera house,
which reopened at the end of 2004 after
a lengthy, and controversial, refurbish-
ment. A visit to the **Museo Teatrale alla
Scala** (daily 9am–12.30pm, 1.30–
5.30pm; charge) allows you to peep into
the fabulously opulent interior. Tracing
the history of opera and theatre in the
city, the museum exhibits memorabilia
of composers including Verdi, Bellini
and Donizetti, as well as hosting temporary exhibitions.

## QUADRILATERO D'ORO

From Piazza della Scala, head northeast
along **Via Manzoni ❹** towards the
world-famous shopping quarter. If it's
time for lunch and you want to follow
in the footsteps of Verdi, Donizetti and
Toscanini, divert to the **Antico Ristorante Boeucc**, see ⑪②, by taking the
first turn on the right, leading to Piazza
Belgioioso. Another Milanese institu-
tion is **Bice**, see ⑪③, further on, in
the heart of the fashion district.

The so-called **Quadrilatero d'Oro
❺** (Golden Quadrangle) is defined by
Via Manzoni, Via Monte Napoleone,
Via della Spiga and Via Sant'Andrea.
All the big names are here, including
Giorgio Armani, Dolce e Gabbana,
Prada, Valentino, Versace, Gianfranco
Ferré, Gucci, Louis Vuitton, Chanel
and many more. (The latest designers
to join the scene are Vivienne West-
wood, Burberry and Paul Smith.)

*Designer Havens*
The stores range from tiny boutiques
to huge emporia where you can spend
the whole day. Armani's flagship
store, at Via Manzoni 31, combines
the full clothes range with furnishings, Armani Libri (books), Armani
Fiori (flowers), Armani Dolci (choco-
lates) and **Armani Nobu**, see ⑪④.

At the intersection of Via Monte
Napoleone and Via Sant'Andrea, call
in at the **Antico Caffè Cova**, see ⑪⑤,
an old-fashioned café and pastry shop.
This famous patissier has been producing panettone and Sachertorte here
since 1817.

After a reviving coffee explore the rest of the Golden Quad, then cross over Via Manzoni for the Via Monte di Pietà and take the second street on the right for the **Via Brera**.

oured of the fashion district, then slink into the bar at the **Four Seasons Hotel** (Via Gesù 8). Set in a frescoed former monastery, this is a glamorous place for an early evening aperitif.

## THE BRERA

Formerly the city's artisan district, this is a chic and picturesque area, with art galleries and alternative bars still providing a colourful hint of the bohemian.

### Brera Art Gallery

The quarter is home to Milan's showcase museum, the **Pinacoteca di Brera** ❻ (Brera Art Gallery; Via Brera 28; www.brera.beniculturali.it; Tue–Sun 8.30am–7.15pm, last entry 6.45pm; charge), with one of the finest collections of Italian masterpieces. The collection spans some six centuries and includes works by Mantegna, Giovanni Bellini, Tintoretto, Veronese and Caravaggio. The two most celebrated works are both in Room XXIV: the *Montefeltro Altarpiece* by Piero della Francesca and the *Marriage of the Virgin* by Raphael.

### Nightlife

The liveliest streets are **Via Brera** (try the Jamaica Bar at no. 26 for a slice of avant-garde life) and **Via Fiori Chiari** which, as night falls, fills with fortune tellers and illegal street traders. On the same street the **Torre di Pisa**, see ⑪⑥, does some great Tuscan steaks.

Alternatively, sample the vibrant nightlife of the trendy **Navigli** canal quarter, southwest of the centre (Porta Genova metro). Or, if you are enamoured of the fashion district

## Food and Drink

### ② ANTICO RISTORANTE BOEUCC
Piazza Belgioioso 2; tel: 02-7602 0224/760 2288; www. boeucc.it; Sun–Fri, Sun dinner only; €€€
The oldest restaurant in Milan, offering classic Milanese cuisine within a fabulous late-17th-century palazzo. Dishes such as *antipastino caldo del pescatore* (hot fish hors d'oeuvre based on a recipe given to the restaurant by Toscanini), saffron-flavoured *risotto alla milanese* and *costolettine di capretto con carciofi* (kid cutlets with artichokes) are served by smart waiters.

### ③ BICE
Via Borgospesso 12; tel: 02-7600 2572; www.bicemilano.it; Jan–Nov Mon–Sat, Dec daily; €€–€€€
This is *the* classic spot for Milanese risotto and celebrity-spotting, serving traditional gourmet cuisine in a bustling atmosphere. If the main menu, ending in a long list of creamy desserts, looks all too much, you can opt for one of the two-course light-lunch menus, with a glass of wine included. Vegetarian meals are available.

### ④ ARMANI NOBU
Via Pisoni 1 (corner of Via Manzoni 31); tel: 02-6231 8645; Mon pm–Sat; €€€
Fashionistas flock here for the fusion cuisine, with Japanese and South American influences. It is part of the Armani emporium and named after the famous Japanese chef Nobuyuki Matsuhisa, who opened the Nobu chain. If you take fright at the prices, try the sushi cocktail bar downstairs.

### ⑤ ANTICO CAFFÈ COVA
Via Monte Napoleone 8; tel: 02-600 0578; €
An elegant, historic *pasticceria/caffè*, ideal for a coffee-and-cake break while you are shopping in the Quadrilatero d'Oro. Specialities are Sachertorte (chocolate cake) and *panettone* (the light Milanese Christmas cake, nowadays eaten at any time of year).

### ⑥ TORRE DI PISA
Via Fiori Chiari 21; tel: 02-874 877; daily, Sat dinner only, closed 3 weeks Aug; €€
A fashionable and long-established Tuscan trattoria located on a lively street of the Brera quarter. The rustic, homely setting remains as it was in the 1960s, full of paintings and bottles of wine.

# DIRECTORY

A user-friendly alphabetical listing of practical information, plus hand-picked hotels and restaurants, clearly organised by area, to suit all budgets and tastes.

# A

## AGE RESTRICTIONS

There is no age limit for alcohol consumption in Italy, but for purchasing alcohol the age limit is 16. (A proposal to increase the purchasing age to 18 was rejected by parliament in 2007.) The age of consent is 16. The minimum age for driving, provided you hold a full licence, is 18.

# B

## BUDGETING

The best-value hotels and restaurants tend to be located away from the lake-fronts. In high season you can expect to pay €120–250 for a comfortable double room with bath, €90–120 in a simple hotel or B&B. Count on €30–60 upwards for a three-course evening meal with wine in a restaurant, and €16 or so for a pizza and beer. Drinks and coffee taken at the bar are a good deal cheaper than those at a table with waiter service. Entrance fees to museums, galleries and gardens range from €1–9; entrance is free for EU citizens under 18 and over 65.

## BUSINESS HOURS

**Banks** are generally open weekdays 8.30am–1.30pm and 3–4pm (afternoon opening times may vary). Banks at airports and main stations usually have longer opening hours and are open at weekends.

**Shops** are traditionally open from Monday–Saturday 9am–1pm and 3.30/ 4–7.30pm, but an increasing number of stores, especially in the cities, are open all day. Resorts such as Stresa and Bellagio notwithstanding, most shops are closed on Sunday, and some also close on Monday morning.

# C

## CLIMATE

Spring, summer and autumn are all good times to visit the lakes, not least due to the fine weather conditions. Ideal months are May, June and September, when it is warm and sunny but not as hot as midsummer and not quite as crowded. April and May are the best months for the blooming of camellias, azaleas and tulips.

The climate can be unpredictable due to differences in altitude and microclimates. In Milan temperatures can soar in summer to well above 30°C (86°F) and the humidity is high – hence the exodus of Milanese to the cooler lakes. October and November are the wettest months in the region but usually include quite a few unexpectedly fine days. Winter tends to be foggy and cold, and is best avoided.

## CRIME AND SAFETY

The lakeside resorts are generally very safe, as are most of the small towns. In Milan keep an eye on possessions, especially in crowded places such as the

Piazza del Duomo and train and bus stations. For insurance purposes, theft and loss must be reported straight away to the police station *(questura)*. In case of theft, take photocopies of flight tickets, driving licence, passport and insurance documents.

## CUSTOMS

Free exchange of non-duty-free goods for personal use is allowed between EU countries. The following are the guidance levels:

**Tobacco**: 3,200 cigarettes, or 400 cigarillos, or 200 cigars, or 1kg of tobacco.

**Spirits**: 10 litres.

**Fortified wine/wine**: 90 litres (not more than 60 litres may be sparkling).

**Beer**: 110 litres.

Those from non-EU countries should refer to their home country's regulating organisation for a current complete list of import restrictions.

# D

## DISABLED TRAVELLERS

**UK**: RADAR, the Royal Association for Disability and Rehabilitation, 12 City Forum, 250 City Road, London EC1V 8AF; tel: 020-7250 3222; www.radar.org.uk.

**US**: Society for Accessible Travel and Hospitality (SATH), 347 Fifth Avenue, Suite 605, New York 10016; tel: 212-447 7284; www.sath.org.

**Italy**: Milano per Tutti, Via Paolo Mantegazza, 20156 Milan; tel: 02-330 2021; www.milanopertutti.it.

# E

## ELECTRICITY

Sockets take two-pin, round-pronged plugs; supplies are 220-volt. UK appliances require an adaptor, US ones a transformer.

## EMBASSIES/CONSULATES

If you lose your passport or need other help, contact your nearest national embassy or consulate.

**Australia**: Australian Consulate General, 3rd floor, Via Borgogna 2, Milan; tel: 02-777 041.

**Canada**: Canadian Consulate General, Via Vittor Pisani 19, Milan; tel: 02-67581.

**New Zealand:** Consulate General, Via Terraggio 17, Milan; tel: 02-7217 0001.

**Republic of Ireland**: Piazza S. Pietro in Gessate 2, Milan; tel: 02-5518 8848.

**UK:** British Consulate, Via San Paolo 7, Milan; tel: 02-723 001.

**US**: US Consulate General, Via Principe Amedeo 2/10, Milan; tel: 02-290 351.

## EMERGENCY NUMBERS

Ambulance: 118; fire: 115; general emergency: 113; police: 112.

# G

## GAY TRAVELLERS

Milan is Italy's gay capital, and other large towns in the region, such as

**Above from far left:** catching the rays on a beach by Lake Garda; sailing tournament; Santa Maria del Monte village *(see p.51)*.

**Left Luggage**
There are left-luggage facilities at all the airports and at Milan's Central Station. Look for the signs 'Deposito Bagagli'.

Brescia, have gay bars and clubs. Elsewhere attitudes are more conservative, and locals do not always tolerate overt displays of affection. The main point of contact is the Milan branch of the Italian gay organisation, Arcigay (www.arcigaymilano.org, only partially translated into English). The website www.gayfriendly.com is a national guide to the gay scene.

# H

## HEALTH

All EU countries have reciprocal arrangements for reclaiming the costs of medical services. UK residents should obtain the EHIC (European Health Insurance Card), available from post offices or online at www.ehic.org.uk. This only covers you for medical care, not for emergency repatriation costs or additional expenses such as accommodation and flights for anyone travelling with you. To cover all eventualities a travel insurance policy is advisable, and for non-EU residents essential.

A pharmacy *(farmacia)* is a good first stop for medical advice. The name of the duty or all-night pharmacy is posted on pharmacy doors.

# I

## INTERNET

Many of the more upmarket hotels offer wi-fi, and others usually have internet facilities for guests' use (often at extra charge). Internet points can otherwise be found in cyber cafés, libraries or in offices with internet access for the public. Tourist offices can supply a list of local internet points. A passport or ID is normally required for internet use.

# L

## LANGUAGE

Staff in hotels and shops in the main resorts usually speak English, but a smattering of Italian will come in useful if you are off the beaten track. For additional useful phrases, see the pull-out map that accompanies this guide.

hello *salve/ciao*
good morning *buongiorno*
good afternoon/evening *buona sera*
good night *buona notte*
goodbye *arrivederci, ciao (informal)*
please/thank you *per favore/grazie*
yes/no *sì/no*
you're welcome *prego*
I would like… *Vorrei…*
today *oggi*
yesterday *ieri*
Do you speak English? *Parla inglese?*
I don't understand. *No capisco.*
I don't know. *Non lo so.*
How much is it? *Quanto costa questo?*
Where is the tourist office?
*Dov'è l'ufficio turistico?*
What time does the train/bus leave?
*A che ora parte il treno/autobus?*
Where can I buy a ticket?
*Dove posso comprare un biglietto?*
Fill it up please.
*Faccia il pieno per favore.*
Can I park here?
*Posso parcheggiare qui?*

Above from far left: Limone sul Garda; harbour at the village of Garda.

## LOST PROPERTY

In the event of lost valuables contact the nearest police station *(questura)*. Milan has an office for lost property *(oggetti smarriti)* at Via Friuli 30 (tel: 02-8845 3907, Italian-speaking only; 8.30am–4pm), and another at Central Station within the left luggage office on the first floor Galleria Partenza (6am–1am).

## MAPS

Tourist offices can normally provide you with free town maps and sketchy regional ones. The Touring Club Italiano (TCI) publishes excellent road and hiking maps.

## MEDIA

**Newspapers**. English and foreign newspapers are available from kiosks of main towns and resorts, usually a day late unless you are in Milan. National newspapers include the Milan-based centre-right daily, *Corriere della Sera*, and its centre-left rival, *La Repubblica*. A good source for news in English, and cheaper than foreign newspapers, is the daily *International Herald Tribune*.

**Television and radio**. Hotels of three stars or more usually provide satellite TV, broadcasting 24-hour English-speaking news channels – but not necessarily many other channels in English. Italian TV, comprising the state-run RAI 1, 2 and 3 channels, along with a large number of private channels, churns out chat-shows, soaps, films and numerous advertisements. The state-run radio stations, RAI 1, 2 and 3, mainly broadcast news, chat and music. For the BBC World Service check its website on www.bbcworld service.com for frequency details.

## MONEY

**Currency**. The unit of currency in Italy is the euro (€), which is divided into 100 cents. Banknotes come in denominations of 500, 200, 100, 50, 20, 10 and 5 euros; coins come in 2 and 1 euros, and 50, 20, 10, 5, 2 and 1 cents.

**Cash machines**. The easiest way to access cash is to use an ATM *(bancomat)* with a Maestro, Cirrus, MasterCard or Visa card and PIN number. ATMs are widespread and have instructions in the main European languages.

**Credit cards**. Major international credit cards are accepted in most hotels, restaurants, stores and supermarkets.

**Exchange offices** *(cambio)*. These tend to charge more commission than banks.

**Traveller's cheques**. Since ATMs and credit cards have become the norm, traveller's cheques are no longer widely accepted.

## POLICE

In an emergency the *carabinieri* can be reached on 112, or you can ring the general emergency number: 113. In the case of stolen goods contact the local police station *(questura)*.

Since 2005 smoking has been banned in indoor public places. This includes bars and restaurants, unless they have a separate area for smokers – which very few do.

## POST

Post offices normally open Mon–Fri 8.15am–2pm, Sat 8.15am–noon or 2pm. Only main post offices in major towns open all day (Mon–Fri). Stamps *(francobolli)* can also be purchased from tobacconists.

## PUBLIC HOLIDAYS

Shops, banks, museums and galleries usually close on the days listed below:

| | |
|---|---|
| 1 Jan | New Year's Day |
| 6 Jan | Epiphany |
| Mar/Apr | Easter |
| Mar/Apr | Easter Monday |
| 25 Apr | Liberation Day |
| 1 May | Labour Day |
| 2 June | Republic Day |
| 15 Aug | Assumption Day |
| 1 Nov | All Saints' Day |
| 8 Dec | Feast of the Immaculate Conception |
| 25 Dec | Christmas Day |
| 26 Dec | St Stephen's Day |

## R

## RELIGION

Like the rest of Italy, the region is primarily Roman Catholic. The Church still plays a major role in the community, although numbers of regular worshippers have been in decline for some years. Milan has congregations of all the main religions. For information visit www.hellomilano.it (go to 'useful information', then click on 'worship').

## T

## TELEPHONES

**Phone numbers**. Whether phoning from abroad or within Italy, the full area code must be used. Toll-free numbers within Italy that begin 800 need no other code. Numbers starting with 0 are land lines, those starting with 3 are mobiles.

**Calling from abroad**. To dial Italy from the UK, dial 00 (international code) + 39 (Italy) + area code + number. To call other countries from Italy, first dial the international code (00), then the country code: Australia 61, Ireland 353, UK 44, US and Canada 1.

The off-peak rate for international calls in Italy is Mon–Sat 10pm–8am, Sun 1pm–Mon 8am. For an English-speaking operator and international reverse-charge calls, dial 170; for international directory enquiries, dial 176.

**Mobile phones**. EU mobile (cell) phones can be used in Italy, but check compatibility before you leave. It may be worth buying an Italian SIM card, available from any mobile-phone shop, if you intend to stay for more than a few weeks. The major networks available are offered by Telecom Italia (TIM), Vodafone and iWind.

**Public phone boxes**. Most public phone boxes are operated with a card *(scheda/ carta telefónica)*, available from telephone offices, tobacconists, newsstands and vending machines. Remember to tear off the corner of the card before use. Some public phones also accept credit cards. Prepaid international telephone

cards (from €5), available at post offices and other outlets, can make calling abroad remarkably cheap.

## TIME DIFFERENCES

Italy is one hour ahead of Greenwich Mean Time (GMT). From the last Sunday in March to the last Sunday in October, clocks are put forward an hour.

## TIPPING

Tipping is not taken for granted in Italy, although a bit extra will always be appreciated. In restaurants 5–10 per cent is customary unless service has been added to the bill. For quick service in bars, leave a coin or two with your till receipt when ordering. Taxi drivers do not expect a tip, but will appreciate it if you round up the fare to the next euro.

## TOURIST INFORMATION

*Around Lake Maggiore*
**Orta San Giulio:** Via Panoramica; tel: 0322-905 163.
**Stresa:** Piazza Marconi 16; tel: 0323-30150.
**Varese:** Via Carrobbio 2; tel: 0332-283 604.

*Around Lake Como*
**Bellagio:** Piazza Mazzini; tel: 031-950 204.
**Como:** Piazza Cavour 17; tel: 031-3300 111.
**Menaggio:** Piazza Garibaldi 8; tel: 0344-32924.

*Around Lake Iseo*
**Bergamo:** Piazzale Marconi; tel: 035-210 204;
Via Gombito 13, Città Alta; tel: 035-242 226;
Orio al Serio airport, tel: 035-320 402.
**Iseo:** Lungolago G. Marconi 2; tel: 030-980 209.

*Around Lake Garda*
**Brescia:** Via dei Musei 32; tel: 030-374 9916.
**Desenzano del Garda:** Via Porto Vecchio; tel: 030-914 1510.
**Gardone Riviera:** Corso Repubblica, 8; tel: 0365-20347.
**Malcesine:** Via Capitanato 6; tel: 045-740 0044.
**Riva del Garda:** Giardini di Porta Orientale 8; tel: 0464-554 444.
**Sirmione:** Viale Marconi 2; tel: 030-916 114/916 245.

*Milan*
19A Piazza del Duomo; tel: 02-7740 4343.

*Tourist Offices Abroad*
**UK:** Italian State Tourist Board (for all regions in the lakes except Trentino), 1 Princes Street, London W1B 8AY; tel: 020-7408 1254; www.italiantourist board.co.uk.
**US:** 630 Fifth Avenue, Suite 1565, New York, NY 10111; tel: 212-245 5618; www.italiantourism.com.
**Canada:** 175 Bloor Street East, Suite 907, South Tower, Toronto, Ontario M4W 3R8; tel: 416-925 4882; www. italiantourism.com.

**Above from far left:** Torbole; villa at Pallanza; Lake Como and Monte di Tremezzo.

**Toilets**
Public toilets are hard to come by. If you use the facilities of cafés and bars, buying a drink will be appreciated – even if it is only a glass of mineral water at the bar.

## TOURS AND GUIDES

Tourist offices, travel agencies and hotels can provide details of tours and guides. For excursions on the lakes consult the ferry company website www.navigazionelaghi.it. Reasonably priced day trips from March to October are offered on all the main lakes, often with the option of a three-course lunch on board.

## TRANSPORT

### Arrival by Air

For British travellers low-cost carrier Ryanair (www.ryanair.com) operates flights from the UK to Bergamo's Orio al Serio airport and 'Verona-Brescia' airport, while easyJet (www.easyjet.com) flies from London Gatwick to Milan's Linate and Malpensa airports. British Airways (www.ba.com) has regular flights from London Heathrow to Linate and Malpensa.

From the US there are direct flights to Milan from main cities, including New York, Boston and Los Angeles.

### Airports

**Malpensa**. Located 50km (31 miles) northwest of Milan, Malpensa airport (www.aeroportimilano.it) is a convenient arrival point for the lakes in the west of the region (Orta, Maggiore, Varese and Como). The airport's Terminal 1 is linked to Milan's Cadorna station by the half-hourly Malpensa Express train (www.ferrovienord.it). Trains run every hour and take around 40 minutes. The Malpensa Shuttle and Malpensa Bus Express provide regular coach services to Milan's Central Station, taking 50–60 minutes.

**Linate**. Situated 10km (6 miles) east of Milan, Linate (www.aeroportimilano.it) is the closest airport to the city, and handles mainly domestic and European flights. The Starfly shuttle operates a half-hourly service to Milan's Central Station, taking 25 minutes; the cheaper no. 73 bus departs every 10 minutes for Piazza San Babila in the city centre.

**Orio al Serio**. Bergamo's Orio al Serio airport, 48km/30 miles northeast of Milan (www.sacbo.it), is convenient for the western lakes, and ideal if you are heading to Lake Iseo. The city of Bergamo is only 5km (3 miles) away, with a bus service departing to the city every half an hour. Two companies, Autostradale and Locatelli Air Pullman, operate half-hourly shuttle buses to Milan's Central Station, an hour away.

**Brescia Montichiari/Gabriele D'Annunzio/Verona Brescia**. Confusingly, Brescia's airport (www.aeroportobrescia.it), lying 20km (12½ miles) southeast of the city, has three different names. (Ryanair misleadingly calls it 'Verona-Brescia', even though Verona's airport is Valerio Catullo.) The airport is worth considering for access to Lake Garda and Lake Iseo.

**Valerio Catullo/Verona-Villafranca**. Verona's airport (www.aeroportoverona.it) is 15km (9½ miles) from Verona, and is handy for the Veneto shore of Lake Garda and excursions to Brescia,

Mantua and Venice. Buses depart for Verona's rail station every 20 minutes.

**Other airports**. Lugano airport is another useful gateway to the Italian Lakes, as are Venice and Treviso.

*Arrival by Rail*

The journey from the UK to Milan, via Paris on Eurostar (www.eurostar. com) and then via Switzerland, takes 15 hours. Milan and Como are well served by trains from Switzerland, Germany and France. If arriving from elsewhere in Italy, there are reliable connections from Turin, Bologna, Florence and Rome, and from within the lakes region. For information in the UK on rail travel, contact Rail Choice (www. railchoice.co.uk) or for rail travel within Italy, visit www.ferroviedellostato.it.

*Arrival by Car*

The quickest route to Milan from the UK channel ports takes a minimum of 12 hours, over a distance of 1,040km (646 miles). For route planning and for details on the cost of petrol, road tolls levied on French and Italian motorways, and the Swiss motorway road tax, visit www.viamichelin.com. Reasonable motorways *(autostrade)* and main roads link the lakes from Turin, Milan, Como, Varese, Bergamo and Brescia. But bear in mind that the city centres and ring roads can be both confusing and congested.

*Transport within the Lakes Region*

**Boats**. Operating on all the main lakes, **ferries** *(battelli)* offer the most enjoy-able and leisurely way of exploring the lakes. **Hydrofoils** *(aliscafi)* or **catamarans** *(catamarani)* are faster than ferries, but more expensive and less fun as passengers are confined to the inside. Tickets for these faster services allow use on ferries but not vice versa. On popular summer routes on the main lakes, the hydrofoils fill up quickly.

Useful **car ferries** *(traghetti)* link Intra and Laveno on Lake Maggiore; Menaggio, Varenna, Cadenabbia and Bellagio on Lake Como; and Toscolano-Maderno to Torri del Benaco and Limone to Malcesine on Lake Garda.

**Timetables** covering all ferries and hydrofoils are available from ferry ticket offices and tourist information offices. Timetables change at least twice a year, but the routes remain quite constant. Ferries normally run from 7am but stop quite early in the evening, and services between 12.30pm and 2.30pm are limited. *(See also margin, right.)*

There is a bewildering variety of **tickets and deals** for the major lakes, so check the options before your first trip. These include an all-day ticket for parts or all of the lake, a single or return ferry ticket, and a ferry ticket that includes entry to (or a price reduction at) major sites. Some boats have a bar; others have a restaurant.

An all-day ticket is the most convenient option, but cost-wise it is worthwhile only for several journeys on the same day. Generally, children under the age of four travel free, 4–12-year-olds are just over half-price. Over-60s from the EU nations are entitled to a 20 per cent reduction on weekdays

**Ferry Timetables**
When you consult ferry timetables, make sure you pick the right ferry for the right day. Unless you are familiar with the leaflets, the differentiation between weekday and Sunday/holiday travel is not immediately obvious – especially on lakes Como and Iseo. To study timetables online in advance of travel see www. navigazionelaghi.it for Maggiore, Como and Garda, and www.navigazione lagoiseo.it for Iseo.

## Motorway Tolls

Tolls are levied on the motorways, but it is worth the relatively small expense to cover ground fast. When you approach the payment barrier, make sure you choose the correct lane. Avoid those headed 'Tessera', which are for locals with season tickets. Lanes marked 'Carte' will accept credit cards; cash lanes are indicated with a hand holding notes and coins.

(with proof of identity). Return boat tickets (excluding catamarans or hydrofoils) tend to be valid for two days.

**Motorboats**. There is little public transport on the lakes after 8pm, so if you want to dine in another resort, you should organise transport for the return trip. Bear in mind that private motorboats are generally far more expensive than land taxis. Some island restaurants might transport diners back to the mainland (for example, from Lake Maggiore's Isola dei Pescatori back to Stresa), others, such as Orta San Giulio and Isola Comacina, have an inexpensive boat service. If you are worried about being stranded, discuss the options with your restaurant. If you are using a motorboat taxi, negotiate a price before setting off.

**Bus**. A reasonably priced bus network links towns and villages along the lakeshores. If you do not have a car, a bus can be the quickest means of reaching some destinations; for example, from Stresa to Lake Orta, and (on Lake Garda) from Desenzano to Sirmione, Salò, Gardone or Limone – all of which are inaccessible by train. Services linking villages are less regular, and some stop very early in the evening.

**Rail**. Milan is the main rail hub for the lakes, with excellent, well-priced services to the main towns across the region. Bergamo, Stresa (Lake Maggiore) and Como (Lake Como) all take around an hour by rail. Lakes Varese and Garda (using the station at Brescia) are also well served by trains. Desenzano, on the Milan–Venice line, is the main terminal on Lake Garda. However, the lakes themselves are better served by ferries and buses.

Intercity, Eurocity or Eurostar trains levy a supplement of at least 30 per cent, and require seat reservations. It is advisable to make a reservation well in advance. Return tickets offer no saving on two singles. Tickets must be stamped in the yellow machines on the platforms before boarding the train. Tickets bought on the train incur a hefty supplement. For information on train travel in Italy, see www.ferroviedellostato.it.

**Land taxis**. Taxi fares are high, and there are additional charges for luggage in the boot (trunk), trips at night and trips on Sundays and holidays. Beware of touts without meters who may approach you at airports (especially Linate) and large train stations. The main squares of the larger towns usually have a taxi rank.

### Car Rental

Car-rental bookings made in advance on the internet work out cheaper than hiring on arrival. Make sure you check all the extras when comparing quotes from different companies. The major car-rental companies have offices in the main cities and airports.

Drivers must present their own national driving licence or one that is internationally recognised. There is an additional charge for an extra driver. Credit-card imprints are taken as a deposit and are usually the only form of

payment acceptable. 'Inclusive' prices do not generally include personal accident insurance or insurance against damage to windscreens, tyres and wheels.

## Driving

**Rules of the road**. Drive on the right; pass on the left. Speed limits in Italy are 50km/h (30mph) in towns and built-up areas, 90km/h (55mph) on main roads and 130km/h (80mph) on motorways. Speeding and other traffic offences are subject to heavy on-the-spot fines.

At roundabouts the traffic from the right has the right of way. Seat belts are compulsory in the front and back, and children should be properly restrained. The use of hand-held mobile telephones while driving is prohibited. The blood alcohol limit is 0.08 per cent, and police occasionally make random breath tests. Lights must be used on motorways, dual carriageways and on all out-of-town roads. Visibility vests and a warning triangle are compulsory.

**Breakdowns**. In case of accident or breakdown call 113 (general emergencies) or the Automobile Club of Italy (ACI) on 116. The club has an efficient 24-hour service which is available to foreign visitors.

**Petrol**. On main roads there are plenty of 24-hour stations with self-service dispensers that accept euro notes and major credit cards, although instructions are usually in Italian only.

**Parking**. Finding a parking space in the centre of lakeside resorts is notoriously tricky. Check your hotel has parking facilities (charges can be quite high) or can recommend a parking lot nearby. Parking in towns is controlled by meters or scratch cards, available from tobacconists and bars. The larger towns have multi-storey car parks. Some free parking is controlled by parking discs (if you have hired a car a disc will be provided).

# V

## VISAS AND PASSPORTS

For citizens of EU countries a valid passport or identity card is all that is required to enter Italy for stays of up to 90 days. Citizens of Australia, New Zealand and the US also require only a valid passport. For stays of over 90 days a visa or residence permit is required.

# W

## WEBSITES

Official tourist board websites:
**www.distrettolaghi.eu** – Lake Orta and the west of Lake Maggiore.
**www.turismo.provincia.varese.it** – province of Varese, including Lake Maggiore's eastern side.
**www.maggiore.ch** – Swiss Lake Maggiore.
**www.lakecomo.com** – Lake Como.
**www.bresciaholiday.com** – Lake Iseo and Franciacorta.
**www.lagodigarda.it** – Lake Garda.
**www.provincia.milano.it/turismo** – province of Milan.

**Above from far left**: the touristy way to get around; young cyclists in Arco; motor boat at Porto Ceresio.

**Women**
Unaccompanied women in the lakes region are unlikely to encounter anything more troublesome than the usual Latin roving eye. In Milan a firm eye should be kept on handbags, and women alone should take care in poorly lit streets out of the city centre.

## Lake Maggiore

### Camin Hotel Colmegna

Via A. Palazzi 1, Luino; tel: 0332-510 855; www.caminhotel.com; €€

A late-18th-century villa, built on a hunting estate and set in a large park with romantic trails and waterfall. Retaining its rustic charm, this family-run hotel has prettily decorated guest rooms, a restaurant specialising in lake fish and a private beach. Two terraces make the most of the lake views. Three apartments are also available.

### Grand Hotel des Iles Borromées

Lungolago Umberto I 67, Stresa; tel: 0323-938 938; www.borromees.it; €€€–€€€€

Stresa's grande dame, this historic waterfront hotel faces the Borromean Islands. The *belle époque* decor is stylishly patrician, if somewhat ponderous. Many of the luxury rooms have fabulous views of the lake and Alps. Facilities include palm-shaded gardens, indoor and outdoor swimming pools, a spa and fitness centre, tennis courts, a helipad and a landing stage for private boats.

### Lido

Viale Libertà 11, Angera; tel: 0331-930 232; www.hotellido.it; €

An engaging two-star villa-hotel with a private beach and good fish restaurant *(see p.34)*. The guest rooms are peaceful and functional.

### Pironi

Via Marconi 35, Cannobio; tel: 0323-70624; www.pironihotel.it; €€

A gem of a hotel, housed in a converted medieval Franciscan monastery. Original features, such as frescoes, vaulted ceilings and medieval columns, have been retained, and guest rooms are all individually furnished with antiques. The old cellars have been transformed into an inviting wine bar.

### Il Porticciolo

Via Fortino 40, Laveno; tel: 0332-667 257; www.ilporticciolo.com; €

A scenic three-star hotel on the lake with views of the Alps across the water. The rooms are comfortable, and there is a fine panoramic fish restaurant that serves lake fish, trout ravioli and scampi risotto.

### Il Sole di Ranco

Piazza Venezia 5, Ranco; tel: 0331-976 507; www.ilsolediranco.it; €€€

Situated 4km (2½ miles) north of Angera, this peaceful family-run four-star villa-hotel has a graceful, restful style, lush grounds and lakeside views. Although the emphasis here is on the gourmet restaurant *(see p.118)*, the hotel has now enlarged to 14 rooms, including luxury suites with lake views. A swimming pool and sauna add to the attractions of this long-established inn.

| Price for a double room for one night with breakfast: | |
|---|---|
| €€€€ | over 350 euros |
| €€€ | 200–350 euros |
| €€ | 130–200 euros |
| € | below 130 euros |

### Verbano

Isola dei Pescatori; tel: 0323-30408; www.hotelverbano.it; €€–€€€

Situated on the Borromean 'Fishermen's Island', this tiny romantic hotel is at its best when the hordes have gone. It has a dozen rooms, each named after a flower and furnished with antiques, plus a fish restaurant, flower-decked lakeside terrace and a private shuttle boat for the evenings when the normal ferry service stops.

### Villa Aminta

Via Sempione Nord 123, Stresa; tel: 0323-933 818; www.villa-aminta.it; €€€€

This ravishing little Art Nouveau hotel was built by an Italian admiral in 1918; it now belongs to The Leading Small Hotels of the World chain. Gourmet fare *(see p.118)*, a new spa and fitness centre and views overlooking the pool and lake are all found here.

*(see p.118)*

### Lake Orta

### Cortese

Via 2 Riviere, Armeno; tel: 0322-999 081; www.cortesehotel.it; €€

Built in 2005, this is a modern four-star hotel in the hills above Lake Orta. Minimalist rooms are well equipped, and there is an open-air swimming pool as well as a good restaurant.

### Leon d'Oro

Piazza Motta, Orta San Giulio; tel: 0332-911 991; www.orta.net/leondoro; €€

A family-run hotel with a romantic setting on the waterfront, overlooking

the island of San Giulio. The bedrooms are small but bright and airy (they were all recently revamped), and many feature good views. There is also a noted restaurant with a terrace.

### Villa Crespi

Via G. Fava 18, Orta San Giulio; tel: 0322-911 902; www.hotelvilla crespi.it; €€€€

This grandiose Moorish folly has atmospheric public rooms as well as personalised bedrooms with canopied beds and whirlpool baths. The *raison d'être* here is the lovely two-Michelin-starred restaurant with sophisticated cuisine *(see p.49)*.

*(see p.49)*

### Varese

### Bologna

Via B. Broggi 7, Varese; tel: 0332-234 362; www.albergobologna.it; €€

A welcoming three-star family-run hotel in the heart of the Old Town, with simple, spacious rooms. Attached is a fine trattoria with specialities from Emilia Romagna, including pasta, salami and antipasti.

### Palace Grand Hotel Varese

Via L. Manara 11, Varese; tel: 0332-327 100; www.palacevarese.it; €€€

This is Varese's top hotel – an Art Nouveau palace set on Mont Campigli, with gorgeous views across the city, lake and hills. The public rooms have a ponderous charm, while suites are spacious. Guests have included Bob Dylan and Catherine Deneuve. There is an haute-cuisine restaurant here, plus gardens, tennis courts, a swimming pool and spa.

**Above from far left:** idyllic lake view at the Grand Hotel Villa d'Este; room and aerial view of Villa Crespi.

**A Wide Range** Accommodation on the lakes is abundant, with grand dowager hotels on the waterfront, romantic retreats in the hills, farmhouses, city-centre designer hotels, and self-catering villas and apartments. Accommodation is not cheap, especially if you choose a lakeside location. Hotels are categorised from one to five stars and five-star de luxe; the stars refer to facilities rather than quality.

## Lake Como

### Le Due Corti

Piazza Vittoria 12/13, Como; tel: 031-328 111; email: hoteldue corti@virgilio.it; €€–€€€

This former monastery and post house has been sensitively converted, despite the pool being placed in what were once the cloisters. The mood is one of quiet good taste, with warm fabrics and exposed beams matched by cosy rooms and a good restaurant.

### Florence

Piazza Mazzini 46, Bellagio; tel: 031-950 342; www.hotelflorence bellagio.it; €€–€€€

A charming traditional hotel that has been in the same family for over 100 years. Public rooms feature a mix of burnished wood panelling and contemporary furniture; bedrooms are warmly inviting and priced according to views. There is a good restaurant, a bar with lakeside terrace and a small spa.

### Garden

Via Armando Diaz 30, Nobiallo di Menaggio (about 1.5km/1 mile north of Menaggio); tel: 0344-31616; www.hotelgarden-menaggio.com; €

This inviting small villa overlooks Lake Como. It has 12 attractive rooms and a very pretty garden.

### Grand Hotel Menaggio

Via IV Novembre 77, Menaggio; tel: 0344-30640; www.grandhotel menaggio.com; €€–€€€

A four-star lakeside hotel with panoramic views and well-equipped bedrooms. The service is good, and facilities include a restaurant, terrace, piano bar, gym, heated pool, gardens, private jetty and parking.

### Grand Hotel Tremezzo

Via Regina 8, Tremezzo; tel: 0344-42491; www.grandhoteltremezzo.com; €€€€

Close to Villa Carlotta on the western shore, this is one of the lake's finest hotels. Built in 1910, it is furnished in Art Nouveau style, and offers tasteful period rooms and terraced grounds dotted with modern sculptures. Facilities include two restaurants, a pool, spa, gym, grass tennis court, private jetty, water-skiing and an infinity pool that looks across the lake to Bellagio.

### Grand Hotel Villa d'Este

Via Regina 40, Cernobbio; tel: 031-3481; www.villadeste.it; €€€€

The undisputed empress of the lake, this sumptuous 16th-century villa has been a hotel since 1873 and features palatial frescoed rooms studded with antiques. Fans praise the professionalism, critics complain of the coldness. Facilities abound, with a Michelin-starred restaurant, luxury spa, nightclub, lake-floating pool, indoor pool, golf, watersports, eight tennis courts, squash-

Price for a double room for one night with breakfast:

| | |
|---|---|
| €€€€ | over 350 euros |
| €€€ | 200–350 euros |
| €€ | 130–200 euros |
| € | below 130 euros |

courts, gym and helipad. This has long been a retreat for the rich and famous, from J.F. Kennedy to Alfred Hitchcock to Madonna. Caroline of Brunswick lived here for five years *(see p.65)*.

### Grand Hotel Villa Serbelloni

Via Roma 1, Bellagio; tel: 031-950 216; www.villaserbelloni.com; €€€€
A luxury hotel comparable with Villa d'Este, with a wealth of marble, crystal chandeliers and frescos. With a Michelin-starred terraced restaurant, state-of-the-art health spa, outdoor pool, children's indoor pool with rocks and water slides, private beach, watersports and tennis, it has everything you could want, plus superb lake views.

### Locanda Sant'Anna

Via Sant'Anna 152, Argegno (on the Schignano road); tel: 031-821 738; www.locandasantanna.net; €
A rural retreat in the hills above Argegno, this family-run inn was once a retreat for Como clergy. There are nine comfortable rustic rooms and a recommended restaurant *(see p.120)*.

### Royal Victoria

Piazza San Giorgio 5, Varenna; tel: 0341-815 111; www.royal victoria.com; €€–€€€
This four-star hotel in the centre of picturesque Varenna has been offering guests hospitality and comfort since the early 19th century. The name changed from the Royal Hotel after Queen Victoria stayed here in 1938. Occupying a prime spot right on the lake, its rooms look across to Bellagio across the water.

The hotel also has an enchanting lakeside terrace where you can dine, and a garden with swimming pool.

## Bergamo

### Agnello d'Oro

Via Gombito 22, Bergamo; tel: 035-249 883; €
This quaint and characterful inn, dating from 1600, is best-known for its regional specialities, but also offers 20 simple and smallish rooms. This is one of the very few hotels in the Città Alta (Upper Town).

## Lake Iseo

### Arabe Fenice

Via Fenice 4, Iseo (1.5km/1 mile northeast of Iseo); tel: 030-982 2004; www.arabafenicehotel.it; €€
A good-value four-star hotel, with fabulous lake views and an excellent restaurant that serves Lombard cuisine and fish specialities, and decent breakfasts too. Nearly all 34 rooms have views, and there is a sunny terrace for meals or drinks in fine weather.

### I Due Roccoli

Via Silvio Bonomelli Est, Colline di Iseo, Polaveno; tel: 030-982 2977; www.idueroccoli.com; €€–€€€
A delightful old villa hotel set in the hills 4km (2½ miles) from Iseo. Low-key elegance is the keynote here, with terracotta floors, exposed fireplaces and airy rooms. The noted restaurant features panoramic views, and its specialities include fresh lake produce, home-made salami and fine Franciacorta wines.

**Above from far left:** Canova Bar at the Grand Hotel Villa d'Este; Grand Hotel Tremezzo.

**Seasonal Variations**
Many of the lake hotels are closed between October and March. In high season (which varies according to hotel, but includes Easter and can go all the way from May through to September), hotels with a restaurant may insist on half-board with stays of no less than three days. Provided you know the hotel has a decent restaurant, half- (or full) board can be very good value.

## Punta dell'Est

Via Ponta 163, Clusane; tel: 030-989 060; www.hotelpuntadellest.com; €–€€

An old-fashioned family-run hotel located beside the ferry landing stage in the fishing hamlet of Clusane. Punta dell'Est's fish restaurant is the place to eat the local speciality of baked tench. Unremarkable rooms are enhanced by lake views and the peaceful sound of water gently lapping the shore.

## Relais Mirabella

Via Mirabella 34, Clusane; tel: 030-989 8051; www.relaismirabella.it; €€

In the hills above Clusane, this four-star converted country hotel enjoys panoramic views of Lake Iseo. Rooms are light and stylish. There is a good restaurant with a terrace, a swimming pool and gardens.

## L'Albereta

Via Vittorio Emanuele II, Erbusco; tel: 030-776 0550; www.albereta.it; €€€€

A villa hotel that showcases the skills of Italy's best-known chef, Gualtiero Marchesi. Set in Franciacorta wine country, it is marble-studded and gilded, exuding a spurious glamour.

Price for a double room for one night with breakfast:

| | |
|---|---|
| €€€€ | over 350 euros |
| €€€ | 200–350 euros |
| €€ | 130–200 euros |
| € | below 130 euros |

A favourite for those with limitless pockets and gourmet tastes. As well as a pool, tennis and spa centre, wine-tasting trips are available.

## Villa Gradoni

Azienda Agricola Villa, Frazione Villa, Monticelli Brusati (8km/5 miles from Iseo); tel: 030-652 329; www.villa-franciacorta.it; €

A rural *agriturismo* run by the Bianchi family, who produce sparkling, red and white Franciacorta wines. The self-contained flats are roomy and comfortable, with exposed beams and stonework.

## Duomo

Lungolago Zanardelli 63, Salò; tel: 0365-21026; www.hotelduomo salo.it; €€

Named after the nearby cathedral, the hotel has a fine setting on Salò's spacious waterfront, good-value guest rooms and an excellent restaurant. Set meals (four courses preceded by a glass of Prosecco) can be enjoyed on the lakeside terrace on a summer's evening.

## Gardesena

Piazza Calderini 20, Torri del Benaco; tel: 045-722 5411; www.hotel-gardesana.com; €€

Given it has hosted the likes of Churchill, Laurence Olivier, Maria Callas and King Juan Carlos I of Spain, this traditional hotel is delightfully low-key, and the rooms are very reasonably priced. The harbourside setting is enchanting, and the hotel's Ristorante Buonricordo *(see p.121)* is unmissable.

## Grand Hotel Fasano

Corso Zanardelli, 190, Gardone Riviera; tel: 0365-290 220; www.ghf.it; €€€–€€€€

Once a hunting lodge, this opulent four-star hotel has lush grounds and old-world grandeur. Guest rooms vary in size, style and outlook, and are priced accordingly. Along with gourmet cuisine, there is a revamped spa, indoor pool and private lakeside beach.

## Laurin

Viale Landi 9, Salò; tel: 0365-22022; www.laurinsalo.com; €€€

This sumptuous Art Nouveau villa, set in gorgeous lake-view grounds, served as the Ministry of Foreign Affairs during Mussolini's puppet regime. A fine dining room is the setting for high-class cuisine, but as in many of the grand lake hotels, bedrooms are a bit of an anticlimax.

## Le Palme

Via Porto 36, Limone sul Garda; tel: 0365-954 705; www.sunhotels. it; €–€€

Set beside the ferry landing stage, this 17th-century waterfront hotel is in a quaint but touristy resort. It has a small pool, a rooftop sun terrace, a restaurant with a weekly gala candlelit dinner, and a bar with live music.

## Villa Cortine Palace Hotel

Via Grotte 6, Sirmione; tel: 030-990 5890; www.hotelvillacortine.com; €€€€

A romantic luxury hotel set in parkland a few minutes' walk from the crowds of Sirmione's historic centre. The neoclassical villa has landscaped gardens with fountains, a pool, tennis courts, watersports, a private jetty with boats to rent and a path to a beach restaurant.

## Villa Fiordaliso

Corso Zanardelli 132, Gardone Riviera; tel: 0365-20158; www.villafiordaliso.it; €€€–€€€€

An exclusive Art Nouveau villa hotel where Mussolini and Clara Petacci once stayed. It has a beautiful lakeside setting and a richly decorated interior, but the real highlight is the restaurant with waterside terrace. *(See also p.90.)*

## Milan

## Antica Locanda dei Mercanti

Via San Tomaso 8, tel: 02-805 4080; www.locanda.it; €€€

Situated close to the Castello Sforzesco, this charming boutique hotel has the cosiness of an old-fashioned inn. Some rooms have rooftop views.

## Antica Locanda Leonardo

Corso Magenta 78, tel: 02-4801 4197; www.leoloc.com; €€

A stylishly restored, idiosyncratic hotel with an inner courtyard and garden. Popular with the fashion crowd.

## Gran Duca di York

Via Moneta, 1; tel: 02-874 863; www.ducadiyork.com; €€€

Close to the Duomo, this is boutique hotel with 33 rooms. It is housed in a stylish 18th-century palazzo. Service is attentive, and this good-value hotel attracts a faithful following.

**Above from far left:** Villa Fiordaliso; Grand Hotel Fasano; hotels by the lake at Sirmione.

**Agriturismi**
Working farms, converted barns or other rural properties that rent out rooms or apartments are known as *agriturismi*. These are an excellent choice for exploring rural regions, and for active holidays such as walking, fishing and cycling. Some *agriturismi* offer breakfast and an evening meal based on home-grown produce. Details of properties are available on www.agri turist.it, www.italy tourist.it and www. agriturismo.net.

### Grotto Sant'Anna

Via Sant'Anna 30, Cannobio;
tel: 0323-70682; Tue–Sun; €€

Along the Cannobina Valley, in the mountains behind Cannobio, this restaurant perches on the edge of a spectacular gorge. The simple menu features delicious meat dishes, excellent pasta, cheeses and home-made desserts. The restaurant is about 10km (6 miles) from Cannobio, and you can hike, bike or go by car.

### Luina

Via Garibaldi 21, Stresa; tel: 0323-30285; Mar–Oct; €

Simple, friendly and good-value restaurant belonging to the Luina Hotel, halfway between the central piazza and the lake. Favourites here are the *cannelloni al forno* and the speciality risotto, which is made to order and well worth the wait. There is a terrace for summer dining.

### Lo Scalo

Piazza Vittorio Emanuele III 32, Cannobio; tel: 0323-71480; closed early Jan–mid-Feb, Mon (except evenings from mid-July–mid-Aug) and Tue lunch; €€€–€€€€

> Price guide for a two-course à la carte dinner for one with half a bottle of house wine:
>
> | | |
> |---|---|
> | €€€€ | over 65 euros |
> | €€€ | 45–65 euros |
> | €€ | 25–45 euros |
> | € | below 25 euros |

This ancient arcaded palazzo, which used to shelter fishing boats, has a large terrace for summer lake-view dining. The elegant restaurant is known for first-class Piedmont cuisine, featuring delicious home-made pastas, fish from the lake, as well as meat dishes.

### Il Sole di Ranco

Piazza Venezia 5, Ranco; tel: 0331-976 507; www.ilsolediranco.it;
closed Mon lunch, summer Tue, Dec and Jan Mon and Tue; €€€€

The Brovelli family has been running the Sole di Ranco inn since 1850. The award-winning restaurant sits right on the lake, with an arbour for summer dining and a newly created winter garden with dining area. Dishes such as brandade of pike, ravioli carbonara, smoked duck, and sturgeon with ginger and ginseng are elegantly presented and served. It is also a hotel with 14 rooms (see p.112).

### Villa Aminta

Via Sempione Nord 123, Stresa;
tel: 0323-933 818; www.villa-aminta.it; Apr–Nov; €€€–€€€€

This villa is a delightful five-star luxury hotel with two alluring restaurants: the large richly decorated Le Isole with a candlelit terrace, which serves light lunches and gourmet set-menu dinners, and the enchanting à la carte Restaurant Mori. Both have gorgeous lake views, encompassing the Borromean Islands, and are justifiably sought after for weddings and private parties.

## Lake Orta

### Al Boeuc

Via Bersani 28, Orta San Giulio; tel: 06-4554 0949; €

Sample a good glass of wine or two accompanied by prosciutto, cheese or *bagna cauda* (crudités in hot olive oil, garlic and anchovy dip). This is the oldest and one of the most atmospheric taverns in town.

### Al Sorriso

Via Roma 18, Soriso; tel: 0322-983 228; Wed–Sun, closed two weeks Jan and two weeks Aug; €€€€

This gastronomic Mecca in the tiny village of Soriso attracts devotees from all over Europe. The outstanding Piedmont and Mediterranean cuisine, which is produced by chef Luisa Valazza, has earned it three Michelin stars – achieved by only five restaurants in the whole of Italy. This is a family-run affair, with an elegant, friendly atmosphere. There are also eight comfy guest rooms should you choose to stay.

## Lake Varese

### Vecchia Riva

Via G. Macchi 146, Schiranna, Lago di Varese; tel: 0332-329 300/335; www.vecchiariva.com; €€

Choose a fine day and sit in the garden, looking out on to the peaceful waters of Lake Varese. The restaurant serves up a fine spread of antipasti (where you can help yourself buffet-style), good fish, risotto and pasta dishes. It is also a hotel with functional modern rooms.

## Lake Como

### L'Altra Riva

Via Regina Vecchia 36, Carate Urio; tel: 031-400 260; €€–€€€

L'Altra Riva has a stylish modern setting right on the lake, sporting a waterfront terrace and a plush interior with white sofas. Home-made pasta, lake fish, salads and decadent desserts are elegantly presented and served.

### Il Cavatappi

Via XX Settembre, Varenna; tel: 0341-815 349; Thur–Tue; €–€€

'The Corkscrew' is a minute eatery, with just five tables, hidden in an alley off the main piazza of Varenna. The cuisine is simple but delicious, the atmosphere cosy and the wine cellar well stocked. Wines are used in certain dishes, such as risotto with red wine and smoked cheese, or beef fillet with red wine and pâté. The owner-cum-chef will talk you through the local lake specialities. Booking advisable.

### Il Gatto Nero

Via Montesanto 69, Cernobbio; tel: 031-512 042; Tue evening–Sun; €€€–€€€€

Rub shoulders with celebrities (this is one of George Clooney's favourites), gaze down on to great lake views, and feast on fish and meat specialities. The 'Black Cat', perched in the hills above Cernobbio, is sumptuously decorated and has soft, mellow lighting and a romantic atmosphere. The food may not be quite all it is cracked up to be, but the setting alone is worth a detour.

**Above from far left:** rowing boats and a restaurant at Piazza Motta by Lake Orta; dining room of Michelin-starred Al Sorriso.

**Opening Times**
Opening times are generally lunch *(pranzo)* 12/ 12.30pm–2/3pm and dinner *(cena)* 7.30/8pm–10pm. In main towns and resorts, restaurants may stay open later – this is often the case with pizzerias. Menus at lunch time are frequently cheaper and lighter than those offered in the evening.

### Prices

Menu prices in the rural hinterland tend to be far lower than those on the lakes, except in fashionable wine-growing areas such as Franciacorta, which is studded with upmarket inns. Restaurant bills will usually include €1–4 per person for bread and cover charge *(pane e coperta)* and sometimes a 10–15 per cent service charge.

## Locanda Sant'Anna

Via Sant'Anna 152 (on the Schignano road), Argegno; tel: 031-821 738; www.locanda santanna.net; June–Sept daily, Oct–May Thur–Tue; €€

A rural retreat in the hills above Argegno. Local dishes such as homemade tortellini, grilled vegetables, lamb, venison, wild boar, salami and Alpine cheeses are served in two adjacent rooms, with a garden setting, and valley and lake views.

## Vecchia Varenna

Via Scoscesa 10, Varenna; tel: 0341-830 793; www.vecchia varenna.it; Feb–Dec Tue–Sun; €€–€€€

Amid an irresistible waterside setting, with lake and mountain views, Vecchia Varenna serves an excellent choice of fish. You can have them stuffed with vegetables and herbs, on a spit, as fish cakes, baked with olives and capers or flavouring risottos. Carnivores are not ignored – there is braised donkey, stewed rabbit, or, for more conventional tastes, steak and pork.

### Brescia Region

## Azienda Agricola al Rocol

Via Provinciale 79, Ome, Franciacorta; tel: 030-685 2542; €

This rustic inn is located on a family-run wine estate and farm. Brescian and Franciacorta dishes served here include *casonsèi* (ravioli with bacon and melted butter), tagliatelle with wild mushrooms, beef with local olive oil, and, in autumn and winter, *polenta e osei*, the

'Brescian lunch' of spit-roasted pork and chicken on polenta. Award-winning wines, olive oil, honey and grappa are all available to buy. Reservation essential.

## Baretto di San Vigilio

Via Castello 1, San Vigilio, Bergamo; tel: 035-253 191; www.baretto.it; daily, closed Mon in Jan, Feb and Nov; €€€–€€€€

At the top of Bergamo's San Vigilio funicular you can sit out on this restaurant's terrace (in summer), enjoying gourmet fare and wonderful views of the Città Alta below. The menu offers a wide selection of home-made dishes. You might start with a salad of red mullet with asparagus and foie gras, or risotto with prawns and courgette flowers, follow with meat or fish, and finish off with a delicious dessert or creamy Brescia cheese. There are also 250 wines to choose from.

## Castello Malvazzi

Via Colle San Giuseppe 1, Brescia; tel: 030-200 4224; www.castello malvezzi.it; closed Mon, Thur, lunch Tue, Wed and Fri, Jan and two weeks in Aug; €€€

The panoramic summer terrace of this 16th-century hunting lodge

---

Price guide for a two-course à la carte dinner for one with half a bottle of house wine:

| | |
|---|---|
| €€€€ | over 65 euros |
| €€€ | 45–65 euros |
| €€ | 25–45 euros |
| € | below 25 euros |

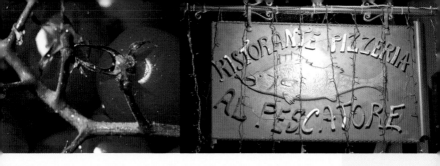

complements excellent cuisine and wines. Booking is essential. The reopened *cantina*, offering *salumi* (cold cuts), cheeses, grilled meat and fish, is open evenings only from Wednesday to Sunday.

## Pizzeria La Bella Napoli

Via Taramelli 7, near Porta Nuova, Bergamo; tel: 035-242 308; Thur–Tue; €

Large and popular pizzeria in the Città Bassa (Lower Town) of Bergamo, catering for all tastes with over 200 types of pizza.

## La Vinera

Via X Giorante 4, Brescia; tel: 030-375 7323; €

An authentic wine bar and inn in the town of Brescia, where you can sample excellent cold cuts and cheeses with recommended regional wines. Informal but informed tasting advice is offered.

Lake Garda

## Agriturismo del Trenta

Via Mazzane 2, Moniga del Garda; tel: 0365-503 395; Sat–Sun only in Feb, Mar, Oct and Dec, closed Nov and Jan; €€

A delightful *agriturismo* with a vine-covered terrace that overlooks the herb gardens and lake. The table d'hôte food is delicious, plentiful and cheap, the staff delightful. Booking essential.

## Alla Campagnola

Via Brunati 11, Salò; tel: 0365-22153; closed Tue lunch; €€€

This welcoming trattoria has a terrace for alfresco meals in the summer, and serves reliable seasonal dishes using home-grown ingredients. Advance booking is advised.

## Buonricordo

Hotel Gardesana, Piazza Calderini 20, Torri del Benaco; tel: 045-722 5411; dinner only, June–Sept daily, Oct and Apr–May Wed–Mon; www.hotel-gardesana.com; €€€

Follow in the footsteps of famous guests *(see p.116)*, and dine by the picturesque old harbour, overlooking the Scaliger castle. The restaurant here offers some of the best cuisine on this side of the lake. Try the delicious *zuppetta di pesci del Garda* (Lake Garda fish soup), the award-winning *filetto di lavarello in agrodolce* (lake fish cooked in a sweet and sour sauce), or *la girella di cavedano al burro e timo* (crêpes stuffed with chub, butter and thyme).

## Caffè Italia

Piazza Malvezzi 19, Desenzano del Garda; tel: 030-914 1243; Tue–Sun; €–€€€

At this well-established café in the centre of the town you can enjoy anything from a morning cappuccino and croissant at the bar, a light lunch on the terrace, or a blow-out seven-course *menu degustazione* (tasting menu). The fish is utterly reliable, and includes French oysters, Sicilian scampi, swordfish and seafood ravioli. This is also a fashionable spot for cocktails and liqueurs.

**Above from far left:** wines produced in the region; a mainstay of Italian cooking; fish is king in the lakes region.

## Vegetarians

Although Italy lags behind the UK in its choice of vegetarian dishes, there are an increasing number of restaurants offering at least one meat-and-fish-free dish. Where there are no main vegetarian dishes on offer, opt for a vegetable-based *antipasto* and *primo* (first course), but check first that stocks used for sauces are meat-free. Fresh, seasonal vegetables, often used to enrich pasta and risotto dishes, include *melanzane* (aubergines/eggplant), *carciofi* (artichokes), *zucchini* (courgettes), *radicchio* (red-leaved chicory), *funghi* (mushrooms) and *porcini* (wild boletus mushrooms).

## Esplanade

Via Lario 10, Desenzano del Garda; tel: 030-914 3361; Thur–Tue; €€€€

Outstanding cuisine and a panoramic lake setting combine to make this one of the most desirable restaurants in the region. Specialities include lasagne with seafood, eel rolls with pickled vegetables and rosemary-flavoured ravioli with duck and goose liver. Desserts are excellent, and there is a huge list of wines to choose from. Formal setting.

## Osteria al Ponte

Via M. Buonarroti 26, Borghetto, Valeggio sul Mincio; tel: 045-637 0074; mid-Feb–mid-Jan Thur–Mon, closed one week June, three weeks Nov; €€€

A long-established *osteria* within a 17th-century farmhouse on the banks of the River Mincio. Try home-made tortellini, cured meats from the farm, freshwater fish, or braised meat dishes, roasts and game. The well-stocked cellar offers around 500 different wines. You can buy cured meats, cheeses and home-made pastas and desserts at the *salumeria* on site.

## Pasticceria Vassalli

Via di San Carlo 82, Salò; tel: 0365-20752; €

Specialising in chocolate, sweets and cakes, this café/*pasticceria* is hard to resist. Among the local favourites are *pan di Salò*, a rich cake made with candied peel and limoncello, a version of the liqueur made from Lake Garda lemons.

## Il Porticciolo

Lungolago Marconi 22, Lazise; tel: 045-758 0254; mid-Feb–mid-Dec Wed–Mon; €€

An inviting family-run lakeside restaurant that serves a vast array of fish and vegetable antipasti, and fresh fish such as grilled eel, risotto with tench and tagliatelle with perch.

## La Terrazza

Via Benaco 14, Torbole; tel: 0464-506 083; June–Sept daily, Apr–May, Oct and Dec–Jan Wed–Mon; €€

The broad lake-view veranda and Ivo Miorelli's inspired regional cuisine make this one of the most appealing restaurants in the northern part of Lake Garda. With ingredients sourced from the lake, specialities include chub ravioli, perch salad, lake sardines and grilled tench. Wash your meal down with a crisp Pinot Grigio or Muller Thurgau. Very good value.

## La Tortuga di Orietta

Via XXIV Maggio 5, Gargnano; tel: 036-571 251; Mar–mid-Nov Wed–Mon dinner only, also lunch Sun Sept–June; €€€

This intimate little restaurant in the historic centre of Gargnano serves exquisite

Price guide for a two-course à la carte dinner for one with half a bottle of house wine:

| | |
|---|---|
| €€€€ | over 65 euros |
| €€€ | 45–65 euros |
| €€ | 25–45 euros |
| € | below 25 euros |

dishes and great wines. Fish (both lake and sea) predominate, but you can also find meat antipasti and main courses such as carpaccio of duck, and lamb with rosemary and thyme. Michelin-starred, with a well-stocked wine cellar.

## Villa Feltrinelli

Via Rimembranze 38, Gargnano; tel: 0365-798 000; www.villa feltrinelli.com; Apr–Oct; €€€€

This lakeside retreat, built in 1892, was home to Mussolini during World War II, and today is a luxury hotel with rich period furnishings. The gourmet French-influenced restaurant is run by one of the region's best chefs.

### Milan

## Cracco Peck

Via Victor Hugo 4; tel: 02-876774; closed Mon lunch, Sat lunch (and all Sat June–Aug), Sun and three weeks Aug; €€€€

Opened in 2000 by the famous Italian chef Carlo Cracco, this gastronomic wonder was awarded two Michelin stars for outstanding innovative cuisine. Specialities include white truffle dishes, saffron risotto and lasagne with foie gras. At much cheaper prices you can try the more informal Italian bar-bistro at nearby Via Cesare Cantu 3, or a takeaway from the super Peck deli *(see p.18)*.

## Joia

Via Panfilo Castaldi 18; tel: 02-295 22124; Sun evening–Fri, closed most of Aug; €€€€

Atypical of meat-eating Milan, Joia specialises in vegetarian haute cuisine

(as well as fish). The setting is contemporary, the clientele hip, the cuisine avant-garde. Capriciously named delicacies include *l'uovo apparente* (the apparent egg), *il tonno e la sua ombra* (tuna fish and its shadow) and *sotto una coltre colorata* (beneath a colourful carpet), which comprises morels, asparagus, lightly spiced courgettes and mint pesto. Book a week ahead.

## Luini

Via Santa Radegonda 16, tel: 02-8646 1917; Mon 10am–3pm, Tue–Sat 10am–8pm; €

Very handy for a quick snack by the Duomo, this famous bakery specialises in *panzerotto*, a freshly made Puglian pastry folded over fillings of tomato and mozzarella, ricotta, ham and spinach. No credit cards.

## Premiata Pizzeria

Alzaia Naviglio Grande 2; tel: 02-8940 0648; Wed–Mon; €

As its name suggests, this is the foremost pizzeria in the Navigli, Milan's cool canal quarter.

## Trattoria Milanese

Via Santa Marta 11; tel: 02-8645 1991; Mon–Fri; €€

In the centre of fashion-conscious Milan, this is one of a few remaining traditional *trattorie*. Since 1919, it has served simple Lombard fare in a warm, friendly atmosphere. Classic dishes are *osso buco* (braised veal shanks) served with polenta, *risotto alla milanese* and *cotoletta alla milanese* (breaded and fried veal). It also serves great seafood.

# CREDITS

**Insight Step by Step Italian Lakes**
**Written by**: Susie Boulton and
Lisa Gerard-Sharp
**Edited by**: Alex Knights
**Series Editor**: Clare Peel
**Cartography Editors**: Zoë Goodwin
and James Macdonald
**Picture Manager**: Steven Lawrence
**Art Editor**: Ian Spick
**Production**: Kenneth Chan
**Photography**: All by APA: Anna Mockford &
Nick Bonetti, and Neil Buchan Grant, except Bill
Wassman/APA 120–1; Glyn Genin/APA 68T,
69TR, 70–1, 70TL, 71B, 97B, 98B, 98TL, 98TR,
99TL, 99TR, 122; Bridgeman Art Library 96–7;
Getty 24T; Istockphoto 30B, 33T, 35TR, 40B,
42T, 45B, 82T; Leonardo 112–13, 112TL,
113TR, 115; Mary Evans 25B; Topfoto 25T.
**Front cover**: main image: 4 Corners; bottom left
and right: Istockphoto.
**Printed by**: Insight Print Services (Pte) Ltd,
38 Joo Koon Road, Singapore  628990
© 2009 Apa Publications GmbH & Co.
Verlag KG (Singapore branch)
*All rights reserved*
First Edition  2009

## DISTRIBUTION

*Worldwide*
**Apa Publications GmbH & Co. Verlag KG
(Singapore branch)**,  38 Joo Koon Road,
Singapore  628990
Tel: (65)  6865  1600
Fax: (65)  6861  6438

*UK and Ireland*
**GeoCenter International Ltd**
Meridian House, Churchill Way West,
Basingstoke, Hampshire, RG21  6YR
Tel: (44)  01256  817  987
Fax: (44)  01256  817  988

*United States*
**Langenscheidt Publishers, Inc.**
36–36  33rd Street,  4th Floor,
Long Island City, NY  11106
Tel: (1)  718  784 0055
Fax: (1)  718  784 0640

*Australia*
**Universal Publishers**
1 Waterloo Road, Macquarie Park, NSW  2113
Tel: (61)  2  9857  3700
Fax: (61)  2  9888  9074

*New Zealand*
**Hema Maps New Zealand Ltd (HNZ)**
Unit 2, 10 Cryers Road,
East Tamaki, Auckland 2013
Tel: (64)  9  273  6459
Fax: (64)  9  273  6479

## CONTACTING THE EDITORS

We would appreciate it if readers would alert us
to errors or outdated information by writing to
us at insight@apaguide.co.uk or Apa Publications,
PO Box  7910, London SE1  1WE, UK.

www.insightguides.com

# INDEX

# Eastern Italian Lakes

0   5 km

0   5 miles

N

## Tours